S0-BJM-312

Teaching the Slow Learner in the Regular Classroom

EDWIN A. GADDIS

Assistant Superintendent
Ottawa (Illinois) Public Schools

Lear Siegler, Inc./Fearon Publishers

Belmont, California

Copyright © 1971,
by Lear Siegler, Inc./Fearon Publishers,
6 Davis Drive, Belmont, California 94002. All rights
reserved. No part of this book may be reproduced by any
means, nor transmitted, nor translated into a machine
language, without written permission from the publisher.

ISBN-0-8224-6905-7

Library of Congress Catalog Card Number: 76-133536

Printed in the United States of America.

Contents

Introduction

Teaching the Slow Learner in the Regular Classroom has been written for teachers, principals, and others who work with children. It has the following objectives:

1. To help in the identification of the true "slow learner"—the most obvious first step in diagnosis and remediation.
2. To summarize the important areas of current knowledge about the nature of mental retardation as it applies to children in school. (The slow learner is often referred to by psychologists as "borderline mentally retarded," although this term has some connotations that make it unsuitable for use with parents and children.)
3. To point out some of the teaching and organizational practices that have been and are being used in schools in an effort to accommodate slow learners in the classroom.
4. To propose a course of action in developing a climate in the classroom and a working relationship between the teacher and the slow learner that will result in greater progress.

5. To help teachers justify in their own minds the necessity for the extra effort and time needed to help the slow learner, and to give the teacher more confidence in her ability to make a real contribution to the child's education.

6. To list materials that have proved to be of value when used in the classroom with slow learners.

This book is the outgrowth of a personal conviction that slow learners are really educable. They can be taught many reading, communication, and arithmetic skills, as well as such social skills as working with and for others and understanding citizenship responsibilities. Slow learners also profit from art, music, drama, and other enrichment activities. It is my belief that for the slow learner, even more so than for normal pupils, a developmental program in the early years is much more successful than a rehabilitative program after they reach adolescence.

I believe in the uniqueness of the individual. This is not merely a philosophical concept I choose to believe; it is something that my experience forces me to believe. The slow learner is a unique person, with the same variety of strengths and weaknesses, the same drives to live and grow, and many of the same aspirations as normal students.

In the schools we affirm that each child is different. Yet, on the basis of our record, it would seem that we do not always reflect this belief in our actions. If we really did believe it, we would not try so hard to make all children alike. We would long ago have broken the rigidity in many educational programs above the primary grades. What a blessing it would be to our society if the whole teaching profession would discard the idea that all learners will come through the educative process learning the same things in the same ways. The slow learner would thus cease to be considered a problem, for he would be accepted and taught as just one more unique individual.

If we did change our point of view, there would also be a basic change in what would be considered the "fundamentals." The proverbial "three Rs" would be assigned a lesser place; for a fundamental, by definition, is something a person just can't do without in life. I am not suggesting that we eliminate the three Rs, but only that they may not be the real life essentials in education. All of us know that it is possible for people to thrive as people with only a minimal mastery of verbal skills.

In contrast, a real fundamental need is that of *belonging*. A sense of belonging results from personal involvement in learning activities. Learning should not be a spectator sport. If the teacher wants results, she should try to get each child involved. It is a well-known fact that interest facilitates learning. The best way to achieve interest is to get involvement and personal commitment from each student.

Another fundamental need is that of *socialization*. As John Donne said, "No man is an island." A newborn infant is helped to become a thinking and feeling human being by his relationship with people. This has been proven by research. The slow learner likewise needs constant contact with his peers. A part of this interaction is communication. The reason why many children act like slow learners is that no one has ever taken the time to talk with them. I have seen far too many slow learners who were allowed to sit day after day in classrooms with only minimal opportunities to recite or participate. Could it be that this is the reason why these children sometimes satisfy the inner drive to communicate by bothering those around them?

A third fundamental need is *love*. Nothing can take the place of love in a child's life. Anthropologists and psychologists tell us that human beings have an innate need for love and a need to respond to love. We might define love as a warm acceptance that allows the one loved to feel secure while preserving his integrity and individuality. It includes some outward show of affection, but a great part of love goes much deeper than this. Some children require frequent reassurance and crave affection; others are more satisfied with a friendly relationship and an expression of interest. If the child does not get love at home, he must find it at school. If he gets love from his teachers and from a few friends, his chances for success are enhanced. An outward "gushy" type of treatment, which some people confuse with love, will not suffice. Nature seems to have given the child a sort of built-in radar, which allows him to detect which people really love him for himself.

Such love will allow him to develop a viable *self-concept,* which is a fourth fundamental need. It must be an honest, useful concept of self, because it must give him the confidence needed to tackle a task on his own. The teacher of the slow learner, if she really loves him, will help him feel bigger, better, and stronger. She will also help him look at his weaknesses without allowing them to overbalance his sense of ableness.

Two more fundamental needs are *creativity* and *freedom*. Like all individuals, the slow learner can grow if he has the opportunity and the encouragement to be creative. More and more we are realizing that creativity is not measured as much by its product as by what it does to the child. Some writers have expressed the thought that creativity is the "soul" of education. In the past we have often been guilty of ignoring this aspect of learning, particularly with our less talented children.

The need for freedom is so basic that there should be no argument about including it in the list of fundamentals. The slow learner must feel free to be himself, to think his own thoughts, and to be accepted as a person. The right to personal freedom must be equated with the need for discipline, however. Any worthwhile educational program requires certain disciplines, some self-imposed, others imposed by those in authority. For the slow learner, who has difficulty with concepts, relationships, generalizations, and cause and effect relationships, an undisciplined atmosphere may prove disastrous. A good teacher should be able to sense the proper relationship between the rights and needs of the individual student and the rights and needs of the group.

Our slow learners can make a tremendous contribution to the future of society. Much of this potential is in the hands of the school, particularly in the early grades. It is hoped that this book will contribute to the unlocking of this potential. It is also my hope that my sincere concern for the child who is considered a slow learner may be reflected in these pages and that this book will prove valuable to those who are working with the slow learner. In conclusion, I wish others the rich reward in personal satisfaction that comes when one sees that his efforts do make a difference.

1

The Problem of the
Slow Learner

Our concern is the child who is not able to keep up with the normal progress of the class, but who is too bright or capable to place in an EMR class. He gets further behind every year, while developing a poorer "self-image" and an increasing distaste for education and all it involves.

Until the last thirty or forty years, educators have taken some unscientific and even inhumane, attitudes toward those children who do not have the abilities to learn readily. Like the rest of society, many schools seemed to follow the principle of "out of sight, out of mind" and just refused to recognize that problem learners existed. Certainly, there was little serious thought about giving them an education suited to their needs. Even now, to some school personnel, the educability of the mentally retarded is a topic about which they have little interest and knowledge. Notwithstanding the tremendous push currently being given to special education, the majority of school districts in this country have little or no facilities or qualified staff to meet the needs of children with special learning problems. Authorities estimate that on the average only one in four slow learners are in special classes. This figure is as low as one in fifty in some states. The deaf, the blind, and the physically or speech handicapped are so obvious that they have received what little attention has been given in most districts, primarily because their needs cry out for attention in a most dramatic way.

Borderline mentally retarded children, whom we shall call "slow learners," are much more numerous in our schools than are the physically handicapped, yet they have received little special attention. Because we did not provide special programs or materials for them, we have been forced, with great harm to them, to channel them into the same educational pattern and curriculum handed down to us from the past—one which we recognize does not adequately fit the needs of the average child, let alone the needs of slow learners. Traditionally, they are put into a self-contained class of thirty or more children, with one teacher, one curriculum, one basic set of tests, and only a minimum of special materials. Then they are evaluated with the same tests and the same questionable grading methods forced upon all children. Even worse, the teacher is generally expected by the administration to put all of the class through the same regimen and then either "pass" or "fail" them at the end of the term.

The common sense of good teachers caused them to see the hopelessness of this practice and encouraged them to start looking for ways to change it. So, teachers, principals, and others improvised as best they could within the existing framework. Often, they had to be teacher, psychologist, psychometrist, counselor, and substitute parent. Recognizing that repeating a grade in the traditional sense would be useless or even harmful to the slow learner, they often resorted to "social promotions" in the belief that it was more important to keep the child with other children approximately his own age than it was to give him further opportunity for success with the skills and subject matter of the present grade. It has been stated quite accurately that about all social promotions accomplish is to keep the children from outgrowing the furniture.

In his book *Instructional Approaches to Slow Learning,* William Younie summarizes some common attitudes toward the slow learner:

> Low achievement is not cultivated or appreciated by society or by its schools. If learning does not reach "normal levels" the teacher

may feel that the child has not been exposed to an advantageous learning situation, is not ready to learn, refuses to learn, or is incapable of learning. Any of the reasons given make the teacher uncomfortable by presenting a direct threat to his professional role. Teachers tend to be measured by the accomplishments of their students, and there is much more reflected glory to be gained from the bright than the dull. Consequently, lack of achievement has a negative connotation. It is not a topic of comfortable conversation.[1]

Organizational Methods

We have had the era of so-called "homogeneous grouping" in which the class was divided into several groups for instruction. These groups were given such fanciful names as "bluebirds, robins, and wrens," or more recently, "astronauts, pilots, and navigators," but the children were not fooled. They had their own blunt names for them— "bright kids, average kids, and dumbbells." All the children who had learning problems were put into a slow class. This might have been beneficial if the classes had been small enough and the teachers had been the best in the school, but the practice was to give the slow classes to poorer teachers or to new, inexperienced teachers. Seldom did the teachers have the required professional knowledge for handling the special problems of these children. Therefore, this often became the dropout class and gradually petered out to nothing shortly before or after the students reached the age of sixteen. Because bright children with learning problems often were put into the same groups, these classes became a breeding ground for social, emotional, and behavior problems. Good teachers would use all the influence they could muster to avoid assignment to these classes. Membership in such a class carried a stigma for the child's parents as well as the child.

Thus the practice of homogeneous grouping, which began with the most idealistic and altruistic motives, sometimes became perverted into a devilish system in which the top group became the "snobs" and the bottom group became the "outcasts." This characterization continued throughout the child's school years and there was little possibility of movement from one class to another.

---

[1]Reprinted with the permission of the publisher from William Younie, *Instructional Approaches to Slow Learning* (New York: Teachers College Press, 1967), p. 3.

The hopeless feeling, which in part was engendered by the system, was perpetuated at higher levels of education. Honor rolls and societies, preferential treatment given to able students, and the strong emphasis placed on going to college have all tended to contribute to the slow learner's feeling of unworthiness and inadequacy. Couple this feeling with the fact that a high percentage of those in the low academic group come from disadvantaged homes and minority groups and you have the ingredients of social unrest.

It would be wrong to say that the majority of the class did not profit from this system, however. But it tended to reinforce the slow learner's already strong conviction of his inadequacy and to contribute to the failure syndrome that characterized his school life.

Forming instructional groups within the class was a step forward — in fact, this technique is still widely used with much benefit, especially where the groups are less rigid and many opportunities are offered for participation and interaction of the whole class. It should be kept in mind that *it is what the slow learner thinks and feels about the grouping that matters.* If he finds the success it affords satisfying enough, the reward may outweigh the stigma of being in the slow group.

Other organizational devices that seem to bring some results with slow children are the continuous progress plan (now called nongraded organization), team teaching, individualized instruction, and classroom helpers. As commonly used, however, these devices still tend to be better adapted to the average and bright pupil than to the slow learner. With him, they are successful only to the extent they deviate from the traditional curriculum and evaluation system. Too often, the changes are organizational only.

We have talked a great deal in education about the "individual child" or about the "child-centered school," but we have not taken much action. We have not been allowed to, or have been unwilling to remake our educational system and redesign our methods to accomplish these ends. Not all the blame should be heaped upon the educator, for the parents and the public have a vested interest in keeping the schools in line with their thinking. A school that dares get too far ahead without taking the parents and public along with its program almost always ends up in trouble. Unfortunately, many school systems don't even try to move forward; it is too easy to conform to the traditional pattern.

In spite of past inadequacies, many sociologists have declared that the schools are the only stabilizing influence available to many children. If we permit early dropout of these pupils, we have denied them this good influence in their lives. It should be perfectly obvious that we can't help them if we don't have them.

Establishing Priorities

Before we can hope to deal adequately with the needs of slow learners, we must meet several priorities:

1. We must distinguish the slow learner from the normal or bright child who has learning disabilities.
2. We must accept the fact that slow learners are educable and can learn many things with proper handling.
3. We must understand and appreciate the pressures put upon the slow learner by the school and strive to keep them from destroying his self-confidence and will to learn.
4. We must use methods and materials suited to the needs of the slow learner, and our instruction must be based upon an adequate theory of learning. All too often a great deal of "teaching" is mechanical and not actually based on any particular learning theory.
5. We must understand that slow learners will be assimilated into our society after leaving school and feel the same obligation to give them the proper foundation for citizenship and social adequacy as we do for other pupils.
6. We must acquaint parents with the needs of slow learners and enlist their understanding and support of the educational program. Without parent and community understanding, progress is difficult.
7. We must have a commitment to provide the extra funds necessary for compensatory education, knowing that we cannot afford to do otherwise. Society pays dearly for every slow learner who does not get the proper education and guidance.

8. We must be willing to change our methodology to suit the needs of the borderline mentally retarded. There must be less dependence on verbal teaching and more on experiences and activities. Slow children are more "thing" minded than normal children. Learning experiences need more concrete reinforcement and less dependence upon involved conceptual processes. Thus, more teaching materials other than books should be used.

9. We must start early, in the preschool years if possible, because many child development authorities are pointing out the crucial nature of this period.

In his book, *A Naturalistic View of Man,* Dr. George Crile states: "There is a critical time in the life of each cell, each organ, each animal, each society, and perhaps in the ecology of the world, at which the organism in question is particularly sensitive to its environment and best able to make an adaptive change. Before or after that time stimulation may be ineffective."[2] He emphasizes the importance of the early years in education and says, "If a choice had to be made between sending a child of mine to nursery school or college, I would pick nursery school."[3]

A number of researchers, including S. A. Kirk at the University of Illinois, suggest that much of our character, attitudes, and values tend to become set or internalized by the age of eight or nine. Buckminster Fuller states that 98% of our environment's positive or negative effects are brought about by the age of thirteen, which is the equivalent of seventh or eighth grade; 80%, by the age of eight; and 50%, by the age of four. If this is true, it means that the earlier we can attack problems that could result in learning disabilities, the better our chances are for success.

The School's Responsibility

Change will have to originate largely with the classroom teachers. They are the ones who deal directly with the child and with whom the child identifies. By fully acquainting themselves with the nature

[2]George Crile, *A Naturalistic View of Man* (New York: Harcourt Brace Jovanovich, Inc., 1969), p. xii.
[3]*Ibid.,* p. 40

and needs of the slow learner and organizing their classroom to accommodate these needs, they offer the best hope we have for success. In most cases they are generally free to organize the classroom as they desire. This is especially true if they have planned carefully and worked everything out in cooperation with the principal or supervisor. It is not necessary to wait until the whole school undergoes restructuring. A complete reorganization may be slow in coming, since there are always segments in the faculty that resist basic changes. Of course, teachers must actively seek the help of their principals, supervisors, school psychologists, counselors, speech therapists, nurses, and all other available resources in their efforts to help the child. The entire resources of the school district should be utilized in the most effective way to overcome the multiple handicaps of the slow learner. When it is realized that they comprise approximately 15% to 20% of the school population, such attention is only logical and morally right.

The school should at all times respect the special parent-child relationship and seek to promote it. Most parents are competent rather than incompetent. Most homes are loving rather than neglectful. The child benefits most when congenial home-school relationships can be maintained and mutual trust and respect are fostered. It is only in unusual circumstances that the school needs to assume a different posture. Taking the child out of the home at an early age is not necessarily the best solution. The "team" approach seems to many to be the better alternative. It has been my experience that the teachers or principals who get along well with parents are also the ones who help children the most. We are wise not to take the pose that the school is always right, and we should always be willing to recognize our weaknesses.

I recall a case that dramatically points out how schools often contribute to, or even create, problems. Because Thomas came into the school from a district that did not have kindergarten, he started out with a disadvantage in first grade. His first grade teacher had been transferred from a fourth grade and had not taught first grade for a number of years. She was unfamiliar with the materials and did a rather poor job of teaching reading the first year, even though she got along well with the pupils. A group intelligence test indicated that Thomas had an IQ above normal, but at the end of grade one he was just getting started well in reading. In second grade, he had a beginning teacher who left the profession at the end of the year because of her inability to handle a class. In many ways, this was a wasted year for Thomas and his classmates. The next three years it just happened that each of the teachers became incapacitated and was absent for several months. The children had a succession of substitute teachers. At this point, Thomas tested only one year behind in reading, but the unfortunate experiences were just too much for him. In spite of a score of 115 on an individual intelligence test, he continued to be a poor student and disliked school. Thomas' classmates who were not so fortunate in terms of mental ability fared even worse. This class was the subject of concern to all and received much special help.

From this experience and others, I have learned that sometimes rather drastic action has to be taken to prevent such a succession of unfortunate experiences for children, for we are responsible if we don't try to minimize them.

2

How To Recognize the True Slow Learner

A simple answer to the question, "Who are the slow learning children?" would seem to be, "Those with I.Q.'s between x and y." But this is not a good answer, for it is too simplistic and fails to take into account many factors. First of all, there is still controversy among the best-informed professionals as to what the I.Q. really is and what it represents in terms of intelligence.

What Is Intelligence?

Some psychologists have classed intelligence as abstract ability or as inherited capacity. Others have taught that intelligence is one's capacity to learn or to adjust and adapt to the total environment. Terman, one of the earliest test makers, felt that intelligence was the ability to think. Some of the more modern concepts of intelligence are broader in nature. Wechsler defines it as the aggregate or global capacity of the individual to act purposefully, think rationally, and to deal effectively with his environment. Erika Fromm holds that intelligence is a function of the total personality. This "dynamic" view of intelligence is the outgrowth of Gestalt and psychoanalytic schools of psychology.

One widely accepted concept of intelligence results from the work of Thorndike and of Guilford. They conceived of intelligence as a hypothetical construct or framework of factors, some of which we may not even know yet.

Thus, intelligence is seen as having many facets. One facet that is being given considerable attention is the adaptive process, which was emphasized by Piaget. He also stressed the developmental nature of intelligence. This has been one of the major contributions to education because it has provided a sound theoretical basis for work in early childhood education. Piaget's theories are gaining wider acceptance since his principles seem to be valid when put into practice. His contribution to the teacher of slow learners lies in the developmental growth theory of intelligence, which helps to explain the reasons for difficulty in cognitive operations and conceptual thinking. The teacher of the slow learner could profit from a review of Piaget's writings.

Group Intelligence Tests

A child's I.Q. is again the center of much controversy, and the pencil-and-paper type of group intelligence test is under suspicion because of its many limitations and weaknesses. This is not to say that it is of no value. Most authorities would agree that a good group intelligence test can serve as one instrument to predict success in school even though it might not measure many facets of intelligence.

The pencil-and-paper type of intelligence test, if properly designed, administered, and evaluated, is also useful for screening a group of children. The scores in the normal range often stand up rather well, even when compared with those from individual tests. The greatest degree of inaccuracy occurs at the extremes, the high and low ends of the scale. Here the pencil-and-paper type of test can be quite unreliable. For these children, the individual psychological examination is a much more valid and reliable tool. It is generally agreed that the group intelligence test is not suitable for the slow learner.

It should be evident that the importance of the I.Q. is not as great as teachers once thought. Some modern writers go so far as to say that an I.Q. is merely the score we get from an I.Q. test. Knowing a child's score on a given test on a given day really doesn't tell the teacher much about the child and his needs. Much other information is needed before the score becomes meaningful.

Some critics of group testing say that the I.Q. can be a "self-realizing prophecy," since some teachers have tended to be influenced by knowing a child's I.Q. In one research project, children having I.Q.'s in the normal range were divided into two equal groups. The teachers of one group were told that the pupils were bright. The teachers of the others were told that the children were dull. At the end of the year, it was found that the children who were in the first group made high grades and the ones in the second group made below normal grades. Such pieces of research do not reflect very highly upon the use of the I.Q. scores by teachers.

I once asked a college class of prospective teachers to list the most important things they needed to know about a child. Almost all placed the I.Q. at the top of the list. There is a reason to question this in light of what we know, or don't know, about intelligence and testing.

In a sense, group tests should be used as a physician uses a thermometer, as an indicator that something is wrong but of little value in specific diagnosis or treatment. So used, along with teacher observation and experience and other measuring devices, group tests are helpful in indicating normality. However, the teacher should avoid using the results of a group intelligence test alone in making important decisions about the slow learner. It would be unwise to label a child as mentally retarded or as a slow learner on the basis of a group test. Such labels should be used with great care, for they tend to stick and to stigmatize. It is because of such abuses of test results that many large school systems have abandoned the use of group intelligence tests.

Another warning should be sounded here. For teaching purposes it is the mental age and not the intelligence quotient that is significant. The MA indicates where the child is in terms of educational level; the I.Q. is a measure of rate that is not particularly significant in planning one's teaching procedure.

Even the MA does not tell the whole story. For example, a boy with an I.Q. of 100 and a chronological age of 7 years would have an MA of 7.0. A boy with a CA of 14 years and an I.Q. of 50 would also have an MA of 7.0. It is obvious that even though both have an MA of 7.0 there will be a great difference in what they know and what they can do. Methodology and materials as well as the teacher's approach would need to be greatly different in helping these two students.

Individual Intelligence Tests

The two most commonly used individual tests of intelligence are the Binet and the Wechsler. Both are largely verbal in nature and are used by psychologists to predict a child's success in school. For this purpose, they seem to be reliable indicators with the normal, the gifted, and the retarded. There is disagreement among psychologists about the ability of even these tests to measure the general intellectual level of the individual, if indeed such a quality can be determined. This is not particularly important, though, since what we really need to know is the child's ability to cope with the school tasks that he will encounter.

Distinguishing Between the Slow Learner and the Learning Disabled

The true slow learner or the borderline mentally retarded child in the regular grade is a low achiever, but not all of the low achievers in a class can properly be classified as slow learners. This distinction is important for identification. Some low achievers are normal or above in intelligence and are more properly called the "learning disabled." Their difficulties may be the result of emotional problems, poor health or nutrition, sensory impairment, brain damage, cultural deprivation, poor motor or visual coordination, or perceptual handicaps of various kinds. These pupils often do rather well in some subjects but poorly in others. Although their school performance may be similar to that of the borderline mentally retarded, these children cannot properly be classified as such. If the teacher has these learning disabled children in the classroom along with the true slow learners, she should be careful to keep in mind the difference and to evaluate and teach them according to their particular needs.

In the case of the true slow learner or the borderline mentally retarded child, the principal contributing factor to poor school work is intellectual subnormality. This may be accompanied by any of the factors listed above. The majority of handicapped children have been found to have more than one isolated disability.

Some educators argue that the simplest way to define a slow learner is to say that he is a pupil who acts like a slow learner. There is some merit in the simplicity of such a definition, but it is over-generalized to the point that it is not realistic. For example, Sara was a child in my school who indicated above-average intelligence and creativity in kindergarten. She had considerable difficulty with beginning reading and language work, however, and at great cost to her personality spent two years in accomplishing what would normally be achieved in one. Thus, if we were to generalize, she would be called a slow learner, although this was definitely not the case. Sara was found to be handicapped by unreasonable pressure from home to achieve, and she had very poor eye, hand, and motor coordination. Once these difficulties were corrected, Sara became a good student and was happy and well-adjusted.

Kent, on the other hand, showed a slowness in maturation in kindergarten. His adjustment to the group was good, but he had difficulty in language, in learning to print his name, and in learning the routines in school. At first, he seemed like a normal boy on the playground, but as the years passed, Kent fell further and further behind in his school work. With much individual help and special materials, he was able to show progress, and he was proud of the work he was able to do. By the time he was a sixth grader his achievement level was about one and one-half years lower than it should have been. Realistically, in Kent's case there was little possibility of his catching up with his class. Kent understood and accepted this; his parents did also, but a little less willingly.

These two children illustrate why it is important to make the distinction between the true slow learner and the learning disabled. The goals and the teaching methods are quite different for the two. Kent and Sara were in the same class. If their teacher had grouped them together for instruction and used the same teaching techniques, neither child's needs would have been met.

Defining Mental Retardation

One helpful definition of mental retardation that can be used in identifying the true slow learner has been adopted by the National Institute of Mental Health and the American Association of Mental Deficiency. It states: "Mental retardation refers to the subaverage general intellectual functioning which originates during the developmental period and is associated with an impairment in adoptive behavior."[1]

Interpreting this definition in terms of the child in the classroom, we can say that "subaverage performance" refers to performance on an accepted individual intelligence test greater than one standard deviation below the performance mean of the age group.

Since the standard deviation on the Binet is 16 I.Q. points and on the Wechsler (WISC) it is 15 I.Q. points, a child must score below 84 on the Binet or 85 on the Wechsler to be considered mentally retarded. Inasmuch as an I.Q. score of 70 to 75 is usually the cutoff for placement in an EMR class, children in the range of 70 to 85 I.Q. would be classed as slow learners. Even children in the upper 80's tend to profit from consideration as slow learners.

These numbers do not represent absolute classifications. The selection of criteria would vary according to the school and the community. For example, in an inner city school where the median I.Q. is below 90 the criteria for the slow learner would be different than in an upper middle-class neighborhood school where the median is over 110. For this reason it is not always wise to place too much emphasis on I.Q.

In general, the "developmental period" mentioned in the definition encompasses prenatal to sixteen years (chronological). The definition also states that there must be an accompanying "impairment in adaptive behavior." This simply means that a child will have shown a slowness in maturational indicators such as sitting, crawling, walking, speech, toilet training, etc. In addition, the child's early learning experiences were slow and/or there was probably an impairment in social adjustments.

---

[1] *A Manual of Terminology and Classification on Mental Retardation,* American Association on Mental Deficiency, Monograph supplement No. 64 (September 1959), Ch. 2, p. 3.

One mistake the classroom teacher is liable to make is to classify a naughty, rebellious, and disturbing child as mentally retarded when a proper individual test would quickly show that this was not the case. Sometimes slow learners exhibit these characteristics, although these actions are no more typical than being withdrawn, shy, overly quiet, or submissive.

The Child's Background

The "typical" slow learner, like the "average" child, is a myth, a statistical entity and not a real person. It is not uncommon to find a pupil who makes a good start in the primary grades and then does poorly later on. This is an important consideration for the middle or upper grade teacher who is planning remedial measures. A close scrutiny of the child's permanent record folder or a conference with his earlier teachers may shed much light on the nature and cause of the problem, but then again it may not.

About the only source of information on the child's preschool years is the parent. Most parents will be quite cooperative if they understand the purposes behind the teacher's questions and have confidence in the school's proper use of any information offered. The parent of a slow learner is more apt to be on the defensive than is the parent of a normal or bright child. It is not easy for some parents to accept the fact that their child is slow. They tend to rationalize by pointing out the areas in which the child's behavior appears more normal. A teacher or principal should use tact and a reassuring manner in questioning parents about maturational indicators, and it should be kept in mind that parent goodwill and cooperation may be of greater importance to the child and to the school than our knowledge of these facts.

It is sometimes true that before the school can reach the child it must reach the parent. A parent who seems difficult may indicate one source of the child's problems. Here is the starting point, then, to attempt to overcome this handicap. A clever teacher or principal can usually break down the barriers between school and home and secure some degree of understanding and cooperation. Only if the attempt is unsuccessful should the school proceed on its own.

The Child's Attitude

Studying the child himself will usually give clues. The slow learner's attitudes toward school are assumed to be negative, but this is not necessarily the case. Many slow learners like school very much, particularly if they have had understanding treatment at school, because it is the only really happy and organized part of their daily life. The school is usually clean, bright, and attractive; there are things to play with, things to do, and room to do something besides watch TV. In addition, it is quiet at school. Children like all of these things, and they may be lacking in their home environment. Many disadvantaged children get security from the routines of the school environment.

Children who do have a dislike for school probably feel this way because of their frustration—expectations are greater than their capacities, or they may not be socially accepted by their peer group. Johnson and Kirk in a study of twenty-five average classrooms found that only about 5% of the mentally retarded children were rated high in acceptance, as compared with about 20% of normal children. Only 4.4% of the normal children were classified by their peers as "rejectees," as compared with 46% of the retarded group.[2]

One of the unfortunate problems of the borderline mentally retarded, in terms of their future school success, is their tendency to have strong feelings of inadequacy and a very poor self-image. Moveover, they often develop a "failure syndrome," in which they become so used to failure that they accept it as inevitable and are unable to succeed at tasks clearly within their capabilities.

Neurological Considerations

Many slow learners have neurological problems including such reactions as poor motor control, hyperactivity, overexcitability, undue anxiety, high distractability, impulsive reaction, and short attention span. Although the classroom teacher may recognize and suspect such symptoms, it would be most unwise for the teacher to attempt a diag-

[2]G. O. Johnson and S. A. Kirk, "Are Mentally Handicapped Children Segregated in the Regular Grades?" *Exceptional Children* (1950), pp. 17, 65–68.

nosis. These neurological factors can only be diagnosed by a competent professional in this field.

Diagnosis should be only the first step, however. To stop there and neglect remediation makes no more sense in education than it would in medicine. It is my opinion that this is often what happens with the diagnostic tests and other devices we administer in school. If we study the findings and develop proper remedial measures, we might not have such a large number of school failures and dropouts.

Neurological conditions may stem from a wide variety of causes, including health, nutritional, or environmental deficiencies. Once the condition itself is diagnosed by a professional, tracking down the origin may not even be relevant to the present problem. For this reason, the main thrust by the school should be in meeting the child's needs *as they find them* rather than in spending much time delving into causes of the conditions. It is debatable whether this is even one of the school's areas of competency, unless it is unusually well-staffed with specialists.

Socioeconomic Factors

Cultural and economic background is another aspect of identification that should be considered. Numerous research studies have shown that the preponderance of the borderline mentally retarded come from homes and communities of low socioeconomic status. One study indicates that 60% of mentally retarded children with I.Q.'s from 70 to 85 come from below-average socioeconomic communities, while 26% to 32% come from average and above-average socioeconomic communities.[3] It is generally true that the child from the deprived home has much poorer experience with language, his experiential background is limited, his attitudes toward learning and school are not as good, and his genetic background is not as favorable.[4]

Since the education level of the parents is usually not high in economically and culturally deprived homes, the verbal handicap is under-

[3]Herbert Goldstein, *The Educable Mentally Retarded Child in the Elementary School,* What Research Says to the Teacher Series, No. 25 (Washington D.C.: Association of Classroom Teachers, a department of the National Education Association, 1962), p. 7.

[4]*Ibid.,* pp. 12-18.

standable. Although they may be quite proficient in the language of their socioeconomic or ethnic community, this language is seldom acceptable in a middle-class-dominated school.

These handicaps may not show up clearly until the second or third grade when the children get into formal instruction in reading, numbers, and language; thus, if we are using academic achievement as our sole criterion to distinguish mentally retarded children, we may be in trouble. Research has indicated that it is most important to get to the mentally retarded's problems before the age of eight or nine.

Studies have also shown that the great majority of elementary teachers come from middle-class backgrounds. There has not been enough emphasis placed on the recruitment of teachers from minority groups and from various socioeconomic groups. As a result, there are few teachers who truly comprehend the culture and the family life of these groups. They have a better understanding of the child who comes from a middle-class home. It is reasonable to believe that a teacher who really understands the background of the disadvantaged child because of unusual empathy or personal experience will be more accepting and understanding and will relate to him and to his parents more easily.

It may be necessary, when teachers are having trouble with a particular student, to examine their relationships for clues. Insignificant details may be causing difficulty. It can well be that the teacher is as much at fault as the child. We all tend to have certain dislikes and prejudices, although they may be well-submerged. Moreover, it is not unknown for a teacher to judge a child by a brother or sister she had in previous years.

Characteristics of a Slow Learner

To summarize, then, there are a number of indicators of moderate mental retardation that the classroom teacher might use, particularly when the services of a competent psychologist are not available. If a child has several of these characteristics, the teacher can assume that he is a true slow learner.

1. The child's scores are very low on a group, pencil-and-paper intelligence test used for screening purposes.

2. The child is a definite underachiever in terms of normal scholastic functioning for a given age. This low achievement characterizes much of the child's school work and not just one or two subjects.
3. The pupil has difficulty with abstract or complex problems or with materials in pattern or sequential order, even though the problems and materials are much below the level normal for his age.
4. The child's maturation record was generally slow. He was late in some of the normal developmental learnings such as crawling, sitting up, standing, speech, feeding habits, toilet training, etc.
5. His environment does not supply the variety and amount of experiences that are needed in learning in school or in developing independence. He has not been encouraged by his environment to work things out, to explore, or to think independently.
6. Social acceptance by his peer group is lower than normal.
7. The socioeconomic level of the home or neighborhood is low.
8. The child has psychological or physiological complications. He may be withdrawn, fearful, and excessively timid, or hyperactive, very aggressive, and difficult to handle. He may have little confidence in himself as a person or in his ability to do assigned tasks. He may dislike school, be unwilling to cooperate, or act abnormally to win attention and affection from others. He may lapse into periods of day-dreaming when he seems to be totally disconnected from the reality around him.

To reiterate, great caution should be exercised in labeling a child as mentally retarded solely because he exhibits some of these behavioral characteristics, for these very same characteristics can be caused in normal and bright children by unsatisfactory backgrounds, home conditions, or neurological problems. They seem to characterize the slow learner only when the other criteria listed above are also present.

A Learning Specialist

Some may ask, "Doesn't all of this take too much of a teacher's time, causing her to neglect the other pupils in the class?" The answer is simply that this is good teaching, and good teaching is not a waste of time. What is more wasteful than trying to teach children something they are not ready to learn or taking time to teach something they already know? Much of this has gone on for generations. We know that the normal and the bright pupil can profitably spend part of the school day in unsupervised independent or small-group learning activities. This gives the teacher the extra minutes needed to devote to individual or small-group help for the slow learners. If we consider that the alternative to giving this special help is to teach the class as if the pupils were all alike, ignoring the slow learners to whom special help is critical, the question of wasted time takes on a different perspective.

The well-trained teacher is a specialist in learning. As such, she seeks to create a climate in the classroom that will facilitate progress on the part of each pupil in the class. She conceives of her curriculum not so much as a body of well-selected subject matter to be taught, but rather as life itself. She tries to keep what she is teaching relevant to the real interests, needs, and abilities of her class. This can be done and still meet all of the traditional requirements for knowledge and skills. As a learning specialist, she recognizes roadblocks to learning and takes the time to overcome them as best she can in order that learning can continue. The good elementary teacher feels as responsible for facilitating progress on the part of the slow learner as she does for challenging the abilities of the bright pupil. Experience seems to bear out the belief that the teacher who keeps her attention focused on her students' needs rather than on the textbook usually teaches more and better in the long run.

As a specialist in learning she understands that self-esteem and self-confidence are essential to learning. With this fact in mind, she never subjects a child to sarcasm or ridicule, nor labels him a failure. On the other hand, she will not overprotect, dominate, or indulge him. She also realizes that every child needs to be challenged to "stretch" his abilities; therefore, she is not hesitant to make him work hard, always keeping the challenge within the limits of his stretching ability. This applies to the gifted and normal pupil as well as to the slow learner.

Good teaching is both an art and a science. The science comes in knowing what should be taught and the best technique for teaching it.

The art comes in the interrelationship between the child and the teacher and in sensing the right course to follow in dealing with conflict. It comes from experience and sincere desire and partly from trial and error. Since teachers' personalities vary, the art of teaching is most difficult to prescribe. It can and must be learned, however, if one is to be a successful teacher. As each of us looks back over our own school years, we realize that there were a few teachers who stood out. In nearly every case, they were highly competent in subject matter and teaching methods, but their strongest feature was how they made us want to do well and to be better than we were. This is the "art" of being a good teacher.

3

Accommodating
the Slow Learner
in the Regular Classroom

At the start of this chapter, let us consider two encouraging facts that have been well-established by research and experience:

1. The I.Q. (as represented by performance on an intelligence test) can be raised significantly, often by as much as 15 to 20 points, by working on special learning handicaps and by placing a deprived child in an environment that is filled with acceptance, rich experiences, encouragement, and plenty of proper health care. When one considers that 15 points could mean a raise from an I.Q. of 80 to an I.Q. of 95, this becomes very significant.
2. The slow learner can and does learn, sometimes surprisingly well. Success and motivation are two important factors in his progress. Failure is its greatest deterrent.

With these two facts in mind, the classroom teacher can proceed with some assurance that her efforts will be rewarded with growth. Progress in school work and social learnings will not be at the same rate as with the normal child, nor perhaps of the same quality, but there will be growth in the educational level of the pupil and in his ability to take care of himself.

The Classroom Setting

Some teachers feel that the only hope for the slow learner is to put them in special classes. This view is encouraged by the fact that the slow learner can sometimes be a problem in the regular classroom if not properly accommodated. However, the research of Jordan and de Charms in 1959 upon testing mentally retarded in special classes and regular classes found a significant difference in favor of the regular classroom.[1] Of course, the teacher will have to give attention to the needs of the borderline mentally retarded pupil in the regular classroom and put forth a definite effort to teach him if he is to be expected to learn. He must not be merely an errand boy.

It would be foolish to argue against the advantages that special classes do have for the slow learner. Generally, the teacher of such a class would be specially trained and have a particular interest. The class load tends to be much smaller, often only 8 to 10 pupils. Nevertheless, isolation of the slow learner from normal pupils does not make for a lifelike situation. Some schools have attempted to overcome this by giving slow learners special help outside the classroom for a portion of the day and then returning them to their peer group for the balance of the day.

Many teachers maintain that cutting down the class load will solve most problems. This would be true if the teacher used the additional time a smaller class gave her to attack the problems of individual pupils. Unfortunately, reducing class size does not necessarily guarantee that individual differences will be considered. There must be an accompanying modification in the way the class is taught.

When such is the case, principals and supervisors have not given teachers the assistance that was needed. It might also be that multilevel teaching materials were not made available to teachers to encourage

---

[1]T. E. Jordan and R. de Charms, "The Achievement Motive in Normal and Mentally Retarded Children," *American Journal of Mental Deficiency* (1959), pp. 64, 457–466.

them to modify their methods for the new situation. Other factors that could play a part are the competition between teachers or classes and an insistence by administrators upon uniformity.

Actually, the significant factor is how the child is handled in the two different settings. It is what you do for the child that matters, not whether he is in a regular or a special class. Obviously, a good special class would be better than a mediocre or poor regular class. All other factors being equal, however, it seems as if the regular, heterogeneous classroom has some advantages.

"Heterogeneous" does not necessarily mean that one must have the entire range of abilities in any given room. Reasonable steps can be taken to limit the range in order to make it possible for one teacher to meet the children's needs. If there were twenty-five or thirty pupils in a classroom and if the range of abilities was from two years below the norm to two years above, and this is not uncommon, the teacher would be faced with a four-year span. Such a teaching situation is not impossible provided that proper materials are supplied, the schedule is arranged appropriately, and there is good supervision and the help of specialists.

In a school where there is only one class for each grade, a teachable range of abilities can be achieved by flexible grouping with a continuous progress plan for each child. The pupil works at his own level and begins the next year just where he left off the year before. Such a program means that one has to ignore traditional grade numbers and throw out the idea that every child in a given room uses the identical set of textbooks. This is not always an easy move to make, because there may be some opposition from parents. The system has been used quite successfully in many schools, however.

If a school has two or more rooms of each grade, there is no reason why each room must include the entire range of abilities. The class membership can be made heterogeneous without encompassing all levels of ability. I have had much success with the following plan: At the end of the school year, each teacher lists her pupils in order of overall competence. She notes those whose work is definitely superior and those who have been working much below grade level. These two groups are not put into the same room. The most able pupils are placed in a room along with pupils on various levels of the average range. The slower students are placed in another room along with a selection of average children. In this way, no teacher will have gifted pupils and slow learners in the same room, although she will still have a good range of abilities. This grouping plan makes it possible for the teacher to have time to do special work with the gifted or slow learners.

This type of grouping has proven to be a fine motivation for some of the average pupils who are in the class with the slow learners. Since they are no longer competing with the gifted pupils, some show talents that they had never demonstrated, or, at least, that had not been observed before. As a result, it sometimes happened that when the classes were made up the following year, some of the pupils who had been listed formerly as average were listed with the superior pupils. The opposite was not true with the average students who were placed with the superior pupils. Fortunately, these students did as well as usual, and they suffered no adverse effects from being the slower group in the room.

If yours is a rather traditional school in which class organization is rigid and retention is the main device for accommodating the slow learner, there is still some hope. In this situation, a teacher should plan each child's extra year for him. This extra year should come after first or second grade. Retention after second grade has so many adverse effects that it should seldom be considered. Perhaps two years of doing first grade work would increase a child's readiness for second grade. If he shows some promise of success at the end of his first year in first grade, he can be moved along into second and spend his extra year in that grade. Although I am not recommending retention as the usual remedy, if at all, in many school situations it may be the only possible move.

One of the worst "crimes" perpetrated against children is making them repeat a grade. This is actually what happens. The child is expected to go over the same course he failed the first time, and, in contrast to retention, no attempt is made to adjust the content and methods to his needs. To do this makes just as much sense as to take a child outdoors and say, "Now, you hurdle that fence." "But I can't get over it," the child may plead. "Then you keep on trying to jump it until you can."

It is encouraging that many schools are abandoning practices that conform the child to the school organization instead of accommodating the school program to the child's real needs. Continued pressure must be exerted to maintain the movement in this direction.

The School's Obligation

The school has a moral obligation to assist the slow learner by developing his capabilities and by helping him acquire skills in basic reading, language, and arithmetic and an understanding of his responsibilities as a citizen. This should be coupled with guidance and counseling to assure mastery of the minimal skills needed to maintain himself profitably in society.

It is a disturbing commentary upon our educational practices that many pupils are slow learners only while they are in a school setting. Out on the playground and in their own homes and neighborhoods they appear to function normally. It seems a little strange that inadequacy shows up only in the classroom. Could it be that what goes on there seems totally unrelated to their personal lives?

We must remember that slow learners do have marketable skills. Most slow learners are capable of being self-supporting and of making a real contribution to society. This is particularly true of those who have been able to profit from a good school relationship. They tend to be average or better citizens, and many make themselves quite indispensable with their talents for service. Follow-up studies made of slow learners have found that upon leaving school, they get jobs, often do rather well, become self-supporting, raise families, and are absorbed into the life of the community.

Although not wishing to characterize any type of work as being appropriate for any given intellectual range, it is true that slow learners tend to enter service occupations. They are often the people who service and repair your car, help with housework, answer your calls for plumbing or electrical work, drive you to work in a cab or a bus, style or cut your hair, paint your house, repair your driveway, or pick up the trash. They may be the ones who cook or serve your food when you dine out and who produce and deliver the foodstuffs we all enjoy. Each of us needs their services badly, and we use them many more hours a day than we do the services of highly trained professionals.

When it comes to citizenship, we should remember that their votes and their taxes count just as much as those of a college graduate. Therefore, we must necessarily be concerned about the slow learner as a person and about his opportunity to get an education that he can utilize. The teacher or the school that plans the school program solely in terms of college preparation is misunderstanding the role of the public school—that of educating all the children of all the people.

The Elements of Learning

In the past, the way classes were conducted seemed to suggest that a child's mind was disengaged from the rest of his life and personality when he entered the classroom. The methods assumed that the child's mind could be broken into parts matching the various class periods in the school day. There was not a widespread understanding that the child's environment; his emotions; his physiological, neurological, and psychological potentialities; and his experiential background played an important role in how much, how well, and how rapidly he learned. Today it can be said that most educators believe this, although their actions in the classroom may not always reflect this belief.

Recently, we have come to realize that one of the most fundamental ways in which retarded children are different from normal children is in the slow rate and inefficiency of their learning. A great deal of the progress that has been made in teaching the retarded has come about in the wake of this realization.

To understand how to teach retarded pupils, one must have some grasp of the basic elements of learning. There is agreement among many psychologists that learning has at least four basic factors: *drive, cue, response,* and *reinforcement.*

Drive might be explained as being the impulse or motivation that causes a person to want to adapt to new stimuli. Hunger and sex are two of the basic drives; and there are many secondary drives such as the desire for acceptance, curiosity, the desire to achieve, etc.

Cue can be thought of as the learning to react appropriately to stimuli. The normal child does this almost instinctively, but the slow learner may be physiologically insensitive to either internal or external cues and thus less likely to heed them. When we look at the tasks the child faces in learning to read or in working with math, we see how important *cue* is and why it is difficult for the child with perceptual difficulties to learn.

Before we can say that a child "learns" something, the essential elements of the correct *response* must be present. For example, vocalization must precede speech; recognition of form and shape must precede reading. A pupil will not learn math, other than perhaps rote counting, until he is able to think symbolically. The child's responses undergo constant refinement and increase sharply as learning takes place, becoming more complex and symbolic. The slow learner, because of his mental dysfunction, is unable to respond as well as the normal child.

Reinforcement is one of the basic elements of learning. It refers to those things we do that increase the likelihood that under given drive and cue conditions the desired response will reoccur. Any reward, whether it is a tangible reinforcer such as a token, or a social reinforcer such as a smile, is considered positive reinforcement. Punishment of any kind is a negative reinforcer. There is still much controversy about the value of punishment, particularly physical punishment, for reinforcement. It should be kept in mind that slow learners, because of their lack of critical thinking ability, may misconstrue the motive back of any punishment they receive.

Learning Theories

When it comes to the how-to-do-it phase of teaching the slow learner, one finds a wide variety of theories and methods. They range from the loving, accepting, free activity type of program advocated by the followers of John Dewey and Carleton Washburne to the highly systematized programs advocated by Newell Kephart and G. N. Getman, and the "pressure cooker" regimentation of the programs of Carl Bereiter and Siegfried Engelmann. Each has its advocates, and each has been shown to have value. At the same time, the opponents of each program have pointed out what they believe to be its weaknesses. The first is accused of being "play school," with entirely too much emphasis on free choice and too much wasted time. Its supporters answer that the other two are regimented, too exclusively directed toward the mechanics of learning, and too destructive of the child's personality.

The average school, however, is not greatly influenced by either extreme. Although there has been an inclination in recent years to lean toward fads, especially those that make good newspaper copy, the mainstream of elementary and secondary education has tended to be conservative. However, the amount of money being spent for new materials and equipment is evidence that schools are not afraid to try new ideas. Whether these changes are only superficial and temporary, or whether they are basic and permanent, remains to be seen. There is no question that more and more educators are taking a long, questioning look at some of the traditional programs and are receptive to new methods that seem to have promise.

Some of the theories about learning and learning disabilities that have made a real contribution to the education of the slow learner will be outlined here. It is hoped that the reader will make a more intensive study of those that seem to meet his or her needs.

Hebb

The theory of D. O. Hebb has come into prominence in the last two decades and has many followers. Hebb's behavioral theory has a peculiar feature: its emphasis upon neurology and perception. He assumes that to a large degree learning is dependent on neural responses to stimuli received by the sense organs. Thus, increasing the stimuli to the senses over a wider area increases the potential for learning. Initial teaching needs to be more "thing" oriented to provide greater opportunity for sensory stimulation and cortical participation.

Hebb's theory points to the need for involving more of the senses in learning. Touching and feeling with whole body involvement should be employed, along with the usual seeing and hearing. Manipulative teaching materials need to be used with young children, particularly the slow learner. Hebb's theory and its emphasis upon neural functioning and sensory perception have opened up a new field of concern, and much new methodology and materials have resulted.

His emphasis on the importance of attention has made us aware of the need to limit the stimulus field of the slow learner so that his attention capabilities may be focused on the task at hand. This is sometimes done by using carrels or "quiet rooms," or by using headphones. It also indicates that in the early stages of learning, the slow learner must be given the opportunity for much experience with simple perceptual stimuli, probably with accompanying specific training in perceptual skills.

Piaget

Another theorist whose work has had a great impact on educational thinking is Jean Piaget. For half a century, he has concentrated on observing children to determine just how they learn. Piaget thinks of intelligence as an "adaptive process" in which the child constantly makes adaptations to his environment and in turn modifies his environment by imposing on it a structure of his own. He conceives of this process of adaptation as the state in which there is equilibrium between the forces that the environment exerts on the learner (accommodation) and those that the learner exerts on the environment (assimiliation). Learning results from the incorporation of sensory data into response patterns called *schemas*. The child practices these schemas and changes or reorganizes them into new response patterns as he learns. In some respects, this idea of organized structures in the central nervous system is similar to Hebb's theory.

Piaget's theories assume that there are definite stages in the development of intelligence that are, in turn, divided into several substages or developmental steps. The three major periods are:

I. The period of sensorimotor intelligence (birth to two years) covers development from natural reflexes such as sucking to the first excursions into the conceptual-symbolic realm.

II. The period of preparation and organization of concrete operations (two to eleven years) in which the child gradually develops a relatively stable and integrated conceptual framework and learns to organize and manipulate his environment. It is the beginning of conceptual and symbolic thinking and a cognitive system that enables him to think of the past, the present, and the future, and to deal with the hypothetical as well as with the real. In this period, he begins to share his social attitudes and his beliefs with others, and to express his feelings.

III. The period of formal operations (eleven years on) in which the individual learns to deal with abstractions, to generalize, and to use the higher thought processes.

Piaget presents a dynamic view of intelligence as an ever-growing, constantly developing power. While not the only developmental theory to be proposed, it is probably the most detailed and viable stage theory we have. It suggests that mental retardation is the result of failure of the child to progress beyond the lower levels of integration.

Piaget's theories are very relevant to the education of the retarded child, even though he did not particularly emphasize individual differences. They reorient our thinking from what a slow learner isn't and what he cannot do, to what he has accomplished and what he may be capable of.

Piaget emphasizes that we learn by doing, that verbalization follows, not precedes, the concept. His theories stress the importance of the continuous interaction of a child and his peers in group activities. He has given us the idea that cognitive development follows in an orderly, sequential pattern that varies to some degree in accordance with the structure of the child's central nervous system and the experience he has gained from the world. This sequence of development applies to the retarded as well as to the normal child..

Couple Piaget's and Hebb's theories about the learning process with the appreciation of the nature of the child as a "totality" rather than as the sum of separate components that the Gestalt psychologists have given us, and the understanding of personality development that we have obtained from the psychoanalytic school of thought, and we have a sound base for understanding the nature and problems of the learner and for programming a sequential learning regime to fit his needs.

Teaching Materials

Kephart

The work of Newell Kephart has had a considerable impact in recent years and seems to contain much of merit. Kephart places the major blame for a child's poor school work on handicaps in a number of perceptual areas. Among these are directionality and laterality, sensory-motor skills, space and form perception, and eye-hand-body coordination. Kephart stresses the unusual requirement for adoptive behavior and stimulus response that a child faces when starting school. He believes that these demands are too great for the child who has a deficiency or impairment of a neurological or physiological process unless special training is given to him. Only then can the child achieve the necessary level of learning readiness or the necessary response plasticity.

Kephart's emphasis upon adoptive behavior, perception, stimulus differentiation, and body image would seem to indicate that his work is based on the Gestalt school of psychology, yet there is a noticeable lack of psychological rationale in his book, *The Slow Learner in the Classroom*. This is not necessarily an indication of weakness in the program. Perhaps, as was true with the earlier work of Maria Montessori, Dr. Kephart found these techniques actually seemed to produce the desired results and was not overly concerned about a complete analysis of why this was true.

The greater portion of his book is devoted to exercises, chalkboard drills, activities with the walking beam, training in form and space perception, and eye exercises. He outlines quite a regimen of play-type activities that can be used to overcome these perceptual handicaps. Teachers who have used them have found that children enjoy them as much as games. Because these methods are being widely used in Head Start and other compensatory programs throughout the country, they are having a wider acceptance in most elementary schools.

It would seem worthwhile for all kindergarten and primary teachers to familiarize themselves with this remedial program and make use of those parts of it that will offer help in overcoming the handicaps they find in their classrooms.

Getman and Kane

A readiness program that is similar in some ways to the Kephart program has been developed in Minneapolis by Drs. Getman and Kane. Formerly called the "Physiology of Readiness" program and published by P.A.S.S. (Program to Accelerate School Success), it is now being published by the Webster division of McGraw-Hill under the title of *Developing Learning Readiness Program.*

Getman's and Kane's primary contention is that the most important time is the readiness period before formal instruction. They also maintain that learning to read, think, and reason have a physiological base. They believe that learning is impossible without movement and that the freedoms and skills of movement come through trial and practice. These freedoms and skills in coordination free the child to interpret the information that comes to him from the world.

Their emphasis upon the readiness period is supported by many authorities. In his book, *Child Development and the Curriculum,* Jersild defines readiness as the "timeliness of what we wish to teach in the light of the child's ability to take it."[2] Huldreth says: "There is a question as to whether we ever teach children anything unless they are interested and willing to learn. A child who is fully ready to learn almost demands to be taught."[3] Itelson and Cantrill state: "Our perceptions give each of us the only world we know. It is this world in which we act. And we act in terms of our perception."[4]

The Getman-Kane program includes sets of games or activities used to develop the following perceptual skills:

1. general coordination
2. balance
3. eye-hand coordination
4. eye movements
5. form recognition
6. visual memory (imagery)

---

[2]Arthur T. Jersild, *Child Development and the Curriculum* (New York: Bureau of Publications, Teachers College, Columbia University, 1946), p. 31.

[3]Gertrude Huldreth, *Readiness for School Beginners* (New York: Harcourt Brace Jovanovich, Inc.), p. 12.

[4]W. H. Itelson and Handley Cantrill, *Perception—a Transitional Approach* (Garden City, N.Y.: Doubleday & Company, Inc., 1954), p. 7.

As with Kephart's work, kindergarten or primary teachers would be wise to secure the teacher's manual for the Getman-Kane program and familiarize themselves with the various exercises, which seem to be just as valuable for the slow learner, perhaps more so, as for the normal child. The whole kit of materials is not so expensive that it is out of reach for many classrooms.

Doman-Delacato

This program, aimed at remediation of serious reading and language cases, has been the center of much controversy. Many recent textbooks in child development and child psychology fail to mention the extensive research done by its authors, Glen J. Doman and Carl H. Delacato. The marked success that some schools have had when using the Doman-Delacato method would indicate that the program cannot be summarily rejected or ignored.

The basic rationale is that the handicaps of poor readers are often a matter of neurological malfunctioning, confusion in "central" dominance, and poor motor coordination. Thus, the handicapped student must be helped, after a careful study of his body behavior, to overcome these neurological and psychological malfunctions before he can learn to read satisfactorily.

The program calls major attention to body mechanics, particularly patterns of creeping and crawling. Eye and hand coordination is also developed. Unlike the Getman and Kane or the Kephart programs, the Doman-Delacato program is not readily available to all schools. It usually requires devoted involvement of the parents, and it is expensive and time-consuming. It is more often found in private schools or in special clinics not associated with schools than in public schools.

Frostig and Horne

Another program of methods and materials that is widely used for overcoming perception problems was developed by Marianne Frostig and David Horne.

The fundamental premise of this program is that perceptual development is basic to all learning. Perceptual handicaps are one of the most frequent sources of learning difficulty and probably the least widely recognized. *Perception* refers to the child's recognition of the world around him. He must rely on what he can perceive through his senses to connect him with other people and with objects. This malfunction is not always caused by physical impairment; faulty interpretation of stimulus can have the same effect.

The child with visual perception disabilities has difficulty in the simplest tasks, even to the extent of inability to participate in games or activities. He has great difficulty in recognizing words and pictures or likenesses and differences. He often gives the impression that he has a low intelligence level or is lazy.

Remediation of perceptual disabilities is important. If this can be done before the child faces formal reading instruction, many school difficulties can be prevented. Perceptual skills are being developed long before the child enters school. A child cannot be expected to realize his individual academic potential unless these skills are developed through normal life activities or taught in his early years in a Head Start program or in nursery, kindergarten, and primary grades by use of perceptual skill-building methods.

The Frostig and Horne methods can be used to train children in five areas:

1. Position in space—relationship of an object to an observer.
2. Spatial relationships—perceiving positions of two or more objects in relation to himself and to each other.
3. Perceptual constancy—seeing the same things in all situations.
4. Visual-motor coordination.
5. Figure-ground perception—distinguishing figures from surrounding stimuli.

The authors of this program maintain that a child who is deficient in any of the five areas probably would be handicapped in all academic work, especially reading. These materials are now called the Frostig Program for the Development of Visual Perception. There are two sets of materials, one for diagnostic purposes and one for remediation.

There is also the Frostig M.G.L. (Move—Grow—Learn) program of sensory-motor training designed to develop movement skills, creativity, body awareness, and other related abilities. These are

enjoyable activities for children and not difficult to teach. This part
of the Frostig program is similar in some ways to the Doman-Delacato
program in that its purpose is to enable children to perceive their
own body schema in relationship to their surroundings.

A "Developmental Test of Visual Perception" is available to use
with children suspected of having visual perception problems, but
this is best administered by a specialist.

Peabody Language Development Kits

Oral language disability is a familiar problem to teachers who work
with slow learners. There seems to have been a delay in the development of communication skills. These "language delayed" children
tend to develop certain types of behavioral traits as a result of their
disability in oral communication. It is sometimes found that they
tend to be rejected by siblings, their peer group, and even by parents
because of this delayed speech. As a result, they can become withdrawn or fearful with some characteristics of autism or schizophrenia.
They often develop negativism and become socially isolated.

The Peabody Kits are excellent teaching materials that were re-
searched and authored by Lloyd M. Dunn, James O. Smith, and
Kathryn B. Horton. Designed specifically to stimulate oral language
and intellectual development, they make it easier for children to
express ideas orally and to understand what others are saying to
them. They have been widely used in regular classrooms, in Head
Start programs, and in compensatory programs for learning disabled or deprived pupils.

These materials, available at a number of levels, can be presented
daily during breaks in the regular school work. No reading or writing
is involved, and no seatwork is necessary. Because the activities are
highly motivating and enjoyable, teachers usually find it easy to get
the participation of all the children in a class or group.

The materials reviewed here represent some of the better known
efforts to develop programs for children with learning problems.
While each is designed to be a program for the remediation of specific
types of learning disabilities, they all seem to have value to most
pupils at certain periods in the learning process. They have been

included here as examples of how increased knowledge about learning and the nature of learning handicaps is affecting what is being done to develop more effective methods and materials.

Teaching Methods

Perhaps the most important point to remember when teaching the slow learner is that instruction should begin at his present functioning level. Every task assigned must be introduced and taught so that success, not failure, will be the probable outcome. The slow learner should not be rushed or pressured; instead, praise and encouragement should be used as incentives. In learning a new skill, the initial steps should be taken slowly with as much repetition as is necessary for mastery. The teacher should keep in mind that the slow learner will not be proficient with abstractions and that long-range goals do not mean much to him. Generally, concrete materials that have short-range goals and an immediate "pay-off" in praise or recognition should be used.

Reading

The teacher must make an effort to secure reading materials on an interest level that will appeal to her pupils. Most eight- or nine-year-old children who read at the first grade level do not want to read the kind of stories commonly found in first grade basic readers. These stories are of great interest to six-year-olds, but are less exciting to older children. Fortunately, a number of companies specialize in high interest and low vocabulary reading materials. There are whole series of such books that do not look like primary books, although they have primary level vocabularies (Fearon Publishers' Pacemaker Books, for example).

The major publishers of basic readers are coming out with "companion" books labeled at the grade level but containing an easier vocabulary. Such books seem to be popular with the students and enable them to do much better and more independent work than ever before. Many companies also have specialized materials including fine seatwork exercises for help with special learning problems.

Researchers who studied the reading success of the slow learner as compared with normal children reported these findings:

1. Both silent and oral reading were performed more effectively by the normal pupils.
2. Slow learners had more difficulty with vowels, more omissions, and inadequate response to more words.
3. Slow learners used context clues less effectively.
4. Slow learners had more visual problems.

It can be seen that slow learners will be less effective in their comprehensional aspects of reading such as appreciation, understanding of figurative or abstract language, drawing inferences, and sequential order. They may not be too deficient at "word calling" and in the use of simple phonics to identify new words. This will enable them to "read" if the material is easy enough.

It is not unusual to find slow learners who are good oral readers, although it may be that their comprehension of what they are reading is not high. Since the modern concept of reading is not word calling but understanding and appreciation of what is being read, it would follow that proficiency in oral reading is not an important evaluation of a child's ability to read. Many excellent readers are poor oral readers, partially because it slows them down and partially because they are so intent on getting the thought that they make mistakes. The slow learner is particularly wary of oral reading if the material is above his mastery level, thus causing him to look foolish because of his frequent mistakes in word calling.

If the slow learner is having trouble with spelling, he can take a shortened version of the weekly test, even if it is only four or five words. In addition to the few words he takes with the class, the slow learner will need drill on a basic word list such as the Dolch list of 220 words. The slow learner should also be taught the various types of skills needed to learn spelling words. Different pupils use different ways to memorize words; no one method, such as phonetics, is enough. Some pupils require the kinesthetic method of tracing the words. Some teachers use a "power" vocabulary list and teach slow learners how many words can be made from root words by adding prefixes and suffixes. As in other subjects, mastery and use of a basic spelling list is better for the slow learner than attempting to learn lists that are not practical for him.

If vocabulary poses a reading problem in any subject, there are several ways to circumvent this. The books can be taken home where an older brother or sister or a parent can read and discuss the passage with the slow learner. Underlining the more important points in the section with pencil helps with review. If a classroom tape recorder with earphones is available, a more able pupil can record the section and then the poor readers can listen and follow along in the book. Even though these techniques will not assure mastery by the slow learner, and although he should not be expected to respond to many of the points, he will get much more than he otherwise would and will not feel left out of the class.

Some teachers locate easy-to-read books on the topics being studied by the class and allow the slow learners to read these in lieu of the textbooks. Most schools will have books with a variety of reading levels on many topics in history, geography, or science. If the slow learner is given easier materials to read, the grade level of the books should not be marked on them.

Arithmetic

Arithmetic can be learned by slow learners in more of a rote manner than by the normal child. Here again, the teacher must use more concrete and less conceptual or abstract methods. If workbooks are available, then content must be taught, just as with other materials. The teacher should not fall into the pitfall of using workbooks as "busy work" for her students.

When one surveys the new math textbooks, it is apparent that more difficult and abstract concepts are being introduced earlier in a child's school years. Many children can master this new material and have an even greater enjoyment of math. It is important to remember, however, that topics that may be exciting and challenging to a good student may be utterly frustrating to a slow learner. He might never master them even if given much additional help and time. At this point we might need to ask ourselves if these concepts and skills fulfill a real need for the slow learner. If they don't, then perhaps we should not spend time trying to teach them. He will do well if he masters the basic content and skills essential to his further learning. We should be pleased with this progress rather than forcing a student to labor over material that he is incapable of grasping.

Team Learning

Another technique that can be used with the slow learner might be called "team learning." A group made up of one or two slower pupils and one or two more able students can be assigned a project or an activity. They work together on it and the final outcome is a joint effort. Short reports or demonstrations can be handled by many slow learners if they have assistance in preparing them. After all there is no valid reason why all activities, even tests, conducted in the class have to be on an individual basis. If the assignment of grades is a problem, perhaps the whole matter of giving grades needs to be reconsidered. Learning, not grades, should be our objective. Since team learning has advantages for the bright pupil, too, it should not be thought of as a drag on them.

These suggestions are applicable in situations where instruction is centered around a textbook in each subject. This is the most commonly found pattern. In classes where there is a multitext or activity program organized around units, it is easier to provide for the participation of all of the class. The more flexible and individualized the instruction, the easier it is to meet the needs of slow learners.

Most teachers are resourceful enough to find ways to involve slow learners in many of the activities of the class and allow them to be participants and not just spectators. While the old practice of letting the slow pupils run errands, clean erasers, empty wastebaskets, straighten the library corner, and do other necessary routine functions still has merit up to a point, it can stigmatize the child in the eyes of his peers. He must also become involved and participate in as many of the large-group activities of the class as possible. This will increase his self-respect and his acceptance by the class.

Emotional and Behavior Problems

In handling the emotional and behavior problems of the slow learner the teacher must be as positive and as creative as possible. Punishment tends to be repressive in nature and is often misunderstood by the slow learner. It may reinforce his already low opinion of himself while not enhancing his love of school. Although the slow learner may need a more structured regimen because of his difficulty with self-control, any reactions by the teacher should contribute to the solution of his problems not add to them.

Herbert Goldstein, in *The Educable Mentally Retarded Child in the Elementary School*, has a very descriptive paragraph about the teacher's attitude:

> ... How does one know whether or not innuendos in statement, act, or mannerism are influencing the pupils and turning them against the retarded child? Do seemingly innocent remarks about the appearance, ability, and behavior of the retarded child serve as a message to the rest of the class that the teacher approves of their acts of rejection? Certainly the teacher must be objective, and he must ask himself how he is affecting the acceptance of the retarded child by the members of the class. The question, however, must be asked as part of the total effort to effect integration of the retarded child in the regular class.[5]

One of the problems of a great many slow learners is their short attention span and their distractability. This is particularly true of those with minimal brain damage. Psychologists point out that attention is especially important for slow learners and more difficult to attain. They cannot learn well if their attention is drawn away from the work at hand every few minutes. For this reason many teachers let their students go to a quiet place to work if one is available. The new trend toward carpeted classrooms and acoustical treatment of walls tends to benefit the easily distracted pupil. The teacher may find that to keep the attention of the slow learner and to keep him working steadily requires more external motivation and devices.

Consider the following list of positive and negative teaching practices that were listed in a statistical review by John Jarolimek.[6] Although they are most appropriate to the teacher of the slow learner, they are also applicable to most teaching at all levels.

Practices that increase hostility:

1. Negative statements by the teacher.
2. Excessively competitive situations.

---

[5]Goldstein, *op cit.*, p. 21.
[6]Reprinted in L. D. Haskew and J. C. McLendon, *This Is Teaching* (Chicago: Scott Foreman and Company, 1962), p. 173.

3. Disregard for individual differences.
4. Rigid schedule and pressure.
5. Highly directive teaching practices.
6. Lack of closeness between the teacher and pupils.

Practices that decrease hostility:

1. Positive statements by the teacher.
2. Successful cooperative class enterprises.
3. Recognition of and adaptations to individual differences.
4. Relaxed, comfortable pace.
5. Pupil involvement in planning and managing the class.
6. Warm and friendly relationship between teacher and pupils.

Summary of Accommodation Methods

Below is a summary of methods that can be used by the teacher to accommodate the slow learner. These points are generally agreed upon by specialists and are successfully practiced in many classrooms.

1. Group slow learners in a flexible rather than a rigid grouping. Keep in mind that the children's special needs, abilities, and interests can be effective bases for grouping.
2. In your teaching, try to get as much feedback as possible. Ask frequent questions to keep a constant check on attention and learning. Draw the pupils out, leading them to right answers. Get the learners to respond and participate; avoid lecturing, because you will quickly lose their interest.
3. Studies show that slow learners can stay with a task for a short time, five to fifteen minutes. Present your material in short periods with a change of activity between.
4. Keep homework to a minimum for the slow learner. You can teach him more effectively at school. This does not rule out certain types of activities that could be carried out at home however.
5. Gear your instruction to the pupils at the lowest level of ability in your class if you are teaching the whole class together. If you teach for the middle or upper level, you will miss the lower level entirely, whereas the reverse is not true.

6. Be careful to isolate concepts, keeping them clear, simple, and direct. Abstractions are difficult, if not impossible, for slow learners.

7. In activities that involve thinking processes, help the pupils think through to the correct answer. Literally steer them along the right course. Avoid having them take a guess.

8. Always keep in mind that your methods must preserve and strengthen the child's self-image. Emphasize success, reward correct responses, and don't react emotionally to an incorrect response. Continually give him evidence of his ability to suceed.

9. Knowing that your slow learners will not be able to cover as much material as normal and bright pupils, concentrate on those aspects of the curriculum that are basic to further progress. It is better for slow learners to master a few skills than to attempt to cover a great many poorly.

10. Remember it is the teacher, not the materials or the curriculum, that is most important to the slow learner. Try to relate to him in the most effective way you can. The teacher sets the stage for the learning that takes place.

At last, we are beginning to succeed with pupils with whom we had always failed. We should all be greatly encouraged by the progress made when proper methods and materials are used with pupils who seem to have almost insurmountable learning problems. Many of those who would not have been considered suitable candidates for high school in the past are now able to complete a modified course without failure and get good jobs after graduation. Many of them are among the best citizens and the most well-adjusted pupils in school. This should be considered a major triumph for their teachers, and it represents a positive answer to those who might ask, "Is it worth all the effort?"

4

Educational Innovations

There is a new spirit in American education today that, hopefully, will bring some much-needed changes. It is a spirit of innovation, experimentation, and adventure. Many people believe changes are coming as the result of the galloping pace of our technology and changing society. There are others who feel that they are coming as the result of the elevation of teaching from a craft to a profession with more ample salaries and better training of teachers. It is essential that these changes be the outgrowth of what we believe, not change for the sake of it.

The task facing educators today is complex; there is the population explosion; the tremendous growth of knowledge in many fields; the belated recognition of the needs of the educationally handicapped and the underprivileged; the increased skill requirements of the labor market; the critical shortage of qualified teachers, particularly in the field of special education; and the scarcity of administrators with the necessary vision, adaptability, and commitment to change.

The changes that are being made are basic ones, not merely minor alterations in methodology or curriculum. Some of the innovations that seem to offer considerable potential for the slow learner will be discussed in this chapter.

Changes in School Design

School building designs are being greatly altered from the traditional plan of long corridors with classrooms lining each side. The buildings are tailored to fit teaching needs, with built-in provisions for convertibility. Learning centers with all types of reference and audiovisual materials are supplanting the library and its collection of books. Science centers, arts and crafts centers, areas for small discussion groups, individual study enclosures equipped with recorders and viewers, areas for dramatics and fine arts, conference rooms, and play areas for free play or group practice of motor-sensory coordination activities are among some of the far-reaching innovations in new buildings. When someone who was accustomed only to the traditional design came into such a building he would be awestruck by the many levels and kinds of activities going on within a given learning area simultaneously.

The flexible scheduling made possible by such facilities offers ample opportunities to provide the slow learner with special attention and remedial work without isolating him from those group activities from which he could profit. He can feel like one of the group and not be conspicuous because of the special help he receives. The very atmosphere of the new educational plant tends to benefit the slow learner. Learning can be more exciting and more motivating. Certain types of activites in which the slow learner's chances of success are greater are more available to him. With this new type of school, we will at last be able to plan the educational program to fit the child's needs instead of forcing him to conform to an outmoded educational plant.

Team Teaching

The continuing exodus of the "egg-carton" type of school, with rows of graded, self-contained classrooms along corridors, has resulted in several new program designs. Team teaching seems to be one of the more promising. Although it had its origin in the secondary school, team teaching is not limited in use to any grade level. It has been proven to be highly successful at the primary level, also.

The system varies from school to school, but the basic plan is for a team of three, four, or five persons to work with a large group of pupils. The size of the group depends upon the size of the team, but a common figure is 60 to 80. The teaching team usually consists of a team leader, two or three teachers, and one or more aides or helpers. The team plans all work together, so that each member becomes familiar with the objectives. During the day, the activities of the pupil group vary from large group sessions in which all are a part to small group and individual work.

Such a plan offers both an economy of time and a greater opportunity for the individual pupil. For example, the entire group may be together to see a movie, hear a talk, see a demonstration, or listen to a concert or drama. Then the group can break down into smaller groups for instruction, discussion, study, or activities that require more personal interaction. Team members have time to offer individual help where needed.

Team teaching has some clear advantages to offer the slow learner since it meets his needs more adequately than the single teacher plan or the departmentalized plan.

1. The day can be divided into more flexible segments, and there is a greater opportunity for individual help.
2. The plan lends itself naturally to the use of materials at different ability levels while keeping the pupils together in an age grouping.
3. Because there are several members of the team, there is a better chance that one or two of the team members will get along well with a particular pupil so that he will be able to relate to someone. In addition, several people will be acquainted with the slow learner's needs and he can benefit from their collective assessment of his problem.
4. Since in a larger group a number of pupils would probably be working at the same level, special help can be achieved more efficiently.

Team teaching requires the participation of a whole school. Since it is a rather drastic change, it should be very carefully planned and staffed. The system will probably not succeed if it is just a matter of changing the schedule. All the staff must understand what is involved and be willing to plan and execute their teaching as a team. Students will adapt to the new plan; for teachers it may take some time. Many experienced teachers, used to the self-contained classroom, may find it a little difficult not to look back to the time when they were king of their own domain.

Team teaching, or some aspect of it, is probably here to stay. It offers a much better way to utilize our new teaching technology than the traditional patterns.

Teaching Machines

A teaching machine is any device that enables a pupil to learn independently by giving him information, questions, and answers. They range from very simple and inexpensive machines up to the extremely expensive computer-type machine. The ordinary flash card that has information on one side and the answer on the other is one of the simplest teaching machines. The language lab equipment commonly used in most schools' foreign language departments would be an example of a more expensive type. There are many others, including booklets into which a student inserts a paper on which the answers are recorded and then checks his answer with that on the paper, and small desk-size machines in which information appears in an opening followed by questions. With this type of machine, the answers appear when the child presses a button or opens a small window.

The importance of the teaching machine is not the machine itself but the programmed learning that goes into it. It is this carefully thought-out program that gives them such potential.

No matter what its form, there are certain advantages to the use of the machine.

1. By their nature they tend to keep the pupil's attention and require him to make a response. He must respond to a question before him.

2. The material can be covered at the child's own pace. Although a bright student might complete the sequence in a few minutes, it is possible for the slow learner to proceed more slowly. The programmed material presented by the machine can be at a level at which the child can succeed. This level must be well below the frustration point.

3. The recall time is not great because the pupil is given one piece of information at a time and is tested on this before he continues. If he is wrong, he can go back, find his error, and try again.

4. Good programmed learning materials are prepared by experts in the subject matter and in the psychology of learning, with the result that the quality of the presentation will tend to be high.

There are limitations to the effectiveness of the teaching machine, however. Although it permits individualization, it may also cause teaching to become quite impersonal. The slow learner responds best to the warm encouragement of a friendly, understanding teacher. A machine under the direction of such a person could be advantageously used.

The teaching machine does its best job with skills and basic factual material. It is much less effective in encouraging creativity or discovery. The idea that the teaching machine could ever replace the human teacher is ridiculous.

One other rather disturbing facet of the development of teaching machines is that they have been produced and sold to parents for use at home. Their advertising claims have been extreme at times, causing parents to spend money that could have been better spent on other types of materials. These claims have raised false hopes that have led to unhappy parents and children.

Auditory Input System

This refers to taped or recorded materials to which slow learners, using headphones, can listen individually or in small groups. Perhaps in the future, visual stimulus will be added through the use of video tapes, filmstrips, or film loops. Since the slow learner needs repetition, and since his reading handicap may prevent him from getting the most out of such subjects as social studies, science, English, literature, etc., where presentation relies heavily on reading, the audio-input systems offers him an opportunity to acquire necessary knowledge by means other than visual. In addition, the material is available for frequent review and for reteaching when necessary for mastery. A clever teacher can find numerous ways to use recorded materials to benefit the slow learner. She may wish to record material herself or have some of her more able pupils make recordings, or she may use some of the excellent taped materials that are being prepared commercially.

Perceptual Development Materials

Some of the better-known materials, such as the Frostig, the Getman-Kane program, and the Peabody Language Kits, were mentioned in Chapter 3. In addition to these materials, many large companies are offering a wide variety of items for perceptual training. Although not much research has been done to date, a great many teachers who use the materials feel that they are of much benefit. They have made it possible for many children who would ordinarily have had trouble with learning to overcome some of their handicaps.

Nongraded Class or Continuous Progress Plan

Although this has been a policy for years in some schools, it would be an innovation in a great many others. In some of the schools that claim to use it, there is not much emphasis on it beyond the second or third grade. With the wealth of published materials now available at every level, there is little excuse for not using this plan. It simply involves giving each pupil lesson materials that are at his own level of ability and on which he has a good chance for success. His grade placement is based more on social and physical factors than on academic considerations so that he does not feel out of place within his class group. Promotion and repeating are strongly deemphasized. The traditional break at the end of the school year is minimized. Any school can institute such a program without a great deal of upheaval if teachers are adaptable and understand and sympathize with the goals. It offers a sound first step in meeting the educational and social needs of individual pupils.

Multitext Teaching

This innovation should be utilized with the preceeding one. The idea is to abandon some of the basal texts and use several different texts at various reading levels. It can be effectively done in most subjects. This system has the advantage of keeping the slow child with the better students, while offering him an opportunity to contribute to the work of the group.

Parent-teacher Conferences

This is a rather common practice in schools today but on a very limited scale. As teachers become more self-confident in handling such conferences, there can be a great deal of parent education as well as good two-way, school-home communication. Whatever the teacher can do to enlist the understanding and cooperation of the parents of slow learners will be much to everyone's benefit. Likewise, the more the teacher knows about the child and his home, the more understanding she can bring to her relationships with him. As parent-teacher conferences are gradually used to supplant or to supplement the formal report card, there will be less negative effect of low grades upon the pupil and the parent.

There should be both planned and informal conferences. The planned conference will come on a regularly scheduled basis—for example, at the opening of school, midyear, and toward the end. At these conferences the teacher should have some of the child's work to show, standardized test results to look over, and questions in mind to ask. The parent should be encouraged to ask questions or volunteer observations or information. Teachers can become quite skillful in conducting these conferences, and much benefit can be derived from them.

The informal conference is not preplanned. It may occur at a PTA meeting, before school or after school, or at other times when parents just drop in. Not too much can be expected of such conferences, and they can even be damaging to the parent-teacher relationship if not carefully handled. Telephone conferences are to be discouraged whenever possible. If there is a problem, it is best talked over privately and face to face. The same applies to chance meetings on the street or in the supermarket with the child present. Such meetings should be as friendly as possible, but it would be advisable to avoid talking about school matters.

Greater Emphasis on Early Education

We are witnessing more and more emphasis being placed on the early years of our pupils. Our Head Start programs have dramatically pointed out the results of reaching deprived children and slow learners as early as possible. Many school problems can be prevented by proper help in the preschool years. Some school districts are trying two-year kindergartens with profit. In this way, the schools offer the slow or immature child a second year of training before starting the formal instructions in first grade, thereby giving him a better chance for success and reducing the chance of retention later on.

Again it should be pointed out that every child's education begins long before school age. All children learn a great deal before they ever reach kindergarten, but some of what is learned may not be beneficial. For this reason, the school needs to serve the community as an instrument for improving early childhood education in the home and neighborhood. The family and neighborhood are "schools" too in this sense. Good teachers and good schools are one of our best hopes for improvement of early education.

Teacher Aides

The use of teacher aides is a promising innovation for all pupils, especially the slow learner. One of the major excuses for not giving the exceptional pupil the necessary special effort is that there simply isn't enough time. Teacher aides, often referred to as paraprofessional personnel, represent an honest attempt to relieve the professional teacher from the time-consuming clerical and routine tasks that are not truly teaching duties.

The teacher aide generally doesn't have a certificate and may not even have college training, but she has skills that are valuable in the school and classroom. Most states allow the use of aides for noninstructional duties. Schools can train them to perform satisfactorily many tasks that teachers have been forced to do in the past because no one was available to do them. Some of the duties that schools have assigned to aides are:

1. Keeping records.
2. Producing duplicated materials.
3. Assisting with audiovisual equipment and in the cataloging, storage, and distribution of films, filmstrips, records, tapes, etc.
4. Assisting in the library with routine duties.
5. Monitoring hallways, playground, or lunchroom.
6. Checking standardized tests.
7. Serving as school receptionist or hospitality aide and directing visitors and students about the building.
8. Assisting teachers with pupils at playground, gym, or dressing rooms.
9. Assisting with art and crafts or music — for example, serving as an accompanist.
10. Reading to students.
11. Locating materials and equipment for teachers.
12. Conducting pupils from classroom to special room or to washrooms.
13. Producing projectuals, charts, or other materials.
14. Assisting pupils in operation of tape recorders, viewers, listening centers, and other educational hardware.

These are necessary tasks that a noncertified individual can do, thus giving the teacher the time she needs to handle the individual and the small group work of the slow learners. Teacher aides should not result in the teacher losing contact with the children. Quite the opposite should be true. They should give the teacher more time for *people* instead of *things*.

New Teaching Hardware

Every month sees more new teaching hardware on the market. Some of the devices could probably best be described as gadgets, but a great deal of them have been well-designed to fill an educational need. They add new dimensions to teaching because they approach learning from other directions than the printed page.

A few of the developments that have already been proven of value are:

1. The tape recorder of the reel-to-reel or cassette type. The uses of the tape recorder seem almost unlimited, and the scope of prerecorded tapes enlarges and improves each year. There have been projects in which each pupil is provided with his own tape recorder to use at home and at school.
2. Overhead projector. This instrument is rapidly becoming a "must" in every classroom. A teacher will be rewarded if she learns to use the overhead. It is a most valuable tool for the slow learner because it can be used to project special drill work, a copy of a test that he needs to take over or spend more time on, and lesson material that he needs to review.
3. Cartridge or film loop projectors. These small, inexpensive machines are widely adaptable to many classroom uses. They can be operated by pupils themselves, and many models do not require a darkened room.
4. Filmstrip viewers. Again, these are small, inexpensive, pupil-operated machines. They make the filmstrip library available to students at any time.
5. Reading improvement machines. Numerous types of machines have been developed for remedial reading, training eye movement, speeding up silent reading, and increasing eye span. They are not hard to operate and offer to the classroom teacher specialized services that might be difficult to secure otherwise.

Modular Scheduling

This is an innovation that will come into greater use as our technology advances. To date, it has been used primarily in large junior high and secondary schools, but there is no reason why it cannot be adapted to elementary school programs. It breaks the school schedule into modules of perhaps 12 to 18 minutes each. Each pupil's school program could thus be very flexible and be tailor-made to his particular abilities and needs.

Modular scheduling contrasts to the traditional school program in which the school day is divided into a number of segments 40 to 50 minutes in length. This rigid schedule seems to be based on the belief that each subject field requires the same amount of time. It tends to waste too much of an able pupil's time and not allow enough flexibility for the slow learners' program.

In contrast, modular scheduling allows some classes to be scheduled for one, two, or even three modules, depending upon the requirements of the instruction. Some classes meet daily; others, less frequently, again depending upon need. The able pupil can take a more varied list of subjects, while the slow learner can have a less demanding schedule.

Schools that have flexible scheduling usually also have some homerooms where pupils who are unable to handle the freedom such schedules permit can learn in a more self-contained, structured setting.

Paperback Books

An innovation that would have shocked teachers a few years ago is gaining great popularity. This is the paperback book (not workbooks). Paperbacks are available at all reading levels and are being published more and more for elementary school use. They cover almost every topic of interest to a child. Here is a readily available tool that can be of use with slow learners. Getting a slow learner to read for recreation is usually difficult, and the paperback could well be the means to this end.

The paperback is even making its way into school libraries where it seems to have a special appeal. School librarians report that poor readers, who shy away from a hardback book, seem to take an interest in the same title in paperback.

There are paperback "book fairs" for children that offer excellent fiction and nonfiction at a very low cost. Schools can even sponsor book fairs at which nothing but paperbacks are sold. Since many children from disadvantaged homes have never had any books or magazines of their own, with the possible exception of comic books, the paperback that can be taken home or that a child can call his own has a special value.

The use of paperback texts is becoming more common in the secondary school and college. More consideration needs to be given to their use in the lower grades.

Educational Television

Television is an educational tool that has almost passed the stage of being an innovation. There is much agreement on the fact that TV has had a considerable impact on this generation. Although some decry the many shortcomings of commercial TV, it would be unwise to say that children have not benefited from it. Unfortunately, the benefits have been minimized by a lack of vision on the part of the industry. Instead of utilizing TV as a device that can open windows to the world, much too often TV networks merely show old westerns, cartoons, inane commercials, and horror movies. This is most unfortunate, especially for the child from a deprived home where TV may be his main contact with the outside world.

Public educational television is becoming more widespread. In addition, many school districts are using either closed circuit (nonbroadcast) television or microwave systems in which the range of the signal is quite limited. Because of these advancements, more classrooms are being equipped with television sets. Video recorders and playback equipment make it possible to use locally produced programs, too.

Educational television and good commercial television have an important value for the slow learner. They enable him to circumvent his reading problem and encounter a much wider and more interesting scope of subject matter than he otherwise would. The appeal to eye, ear, and emotions has a definite advantage. The success of "Sesame Street" will hopefully accelerate the interest in quality educational TV programs and call attention to the potential that television has for education.

The effectiveness of TV in the classroom partly depends upon the cooperation between the TV teacher, who probably is a "master teacher" in the subject, and the classroom teacher, who must follow up the lesson. There must be follow-up to realize the lesson's full value. In most instances, the classroom teacher will have a complete outline of the lesson to be taught by the TV teacher so she can plan this follow-up carefully.

Many educational TV lessons are prepared so that the pupils respond to questions asked by the TV teacher. This has been done effectively in programs at the preschool and primary level and with elementary foreign language. As we gain more experience with various techniques, further improvements will be made in the effectiveness of TV classes.

One definite advantage of TV teaching is that outstanding video-taped lessons developed in one school system can be sold to other districts and used year after year. In no other way can this be done. Thus, the work of our "master teachers" can serve thousands of children.

Learning Materials Centers

The learning materials center is an advanced version of the school library. The difference is not only in the nature of the materials, but also in the way it is housed, used, equipped, and staffed. The modern materials center is an "action focus," where children and teachers come to get far more than just a book or magazine.

In addition to traditional librarian training, the director of a good learning materials center has skill with audiovisuals, thorough knowledge of curriculum, ability to work directly with groups of children, and a knowledge of how children learn. In this sense the director is a real specialist and can be of great assistance to the faculty and students.

The slow learner has an important stake in the development of learning materials centers. We are increasingly aware that how much children learn in the elementary school is definitely restricted if the major emphasis is placed on reading as a means of getting information. For the slow learner, only the simplest dimensions of a concept come through from the printed page, primarily because of the child's limited sight vocabulary and the necessity for exceedingly basic sentence structure.

However, if concepts can be presented pictorially or by sound, he will gain more insight into the material. This has been proven by the way children learn about travel, space science, and many other topics from TV, picture books, tapes, or records. A materials center has books on each topic at various reading levels, magazines, sets of pictures, slides, filmstrips, films, prerecorded tapes or cartridges, charts, models, and a wealth of all types of learning materials that meet the needs of learners at all levels. In addition, there is supervision for the child and assistance in locating and using these materials.

The learning materials center lends itself to the nongraded type of school organization or to any organizational scheme in which children are taught at their own level. The nature of the center makes it more attractive to the slow learner to whom the traditional library could seem foreboding.

Some of the advantages of the learning materials center are available to small schools that are unable to have a separate facility with a fulltime director. There have been many examples of small schools organizing a central library and adding audiovisual materials such as records and record players, tapes and tape recorders, listening centers, filmstrips and viewers, and film loops and projectors at a rather nominal cost. Regular school personnel assist in the supervision and acquisition of materials, and teacher aides help the pupils. Such a facility in a school, while not having some of the important advantages of a regular center, can still make a real contribution toward supplying needed individual help.

When one observes a well-planned and well-staffed learning materials center in operation, the impression is gained that this might well be the prototype for the classroom of the future.

Use of Specialists

In recent years, there has been an increase in the availability of educational specialists—speech therapists, specialists in perceptual training, reading specialists, psychologists, school counselors, and consultants in subject matter fields and audiovisual techniques. These services are vital in dealing with pupils who have special problems. The specialists not only assist the teacher but may also work directly with the pupils who need their services. As the financing of education becomes more adequate and as people recognize that many pupils require special help, we will witness even greater use of various school specialists.

One problem encountered is that some teachers are hesitant to use the specialists who are available. This is most unfair to those pupils who need their services and represents a basic lack of understanding on the part of such teachers.

These are some of the more promising innovations that offer hope for the slow learner. They all represent basic changes rather than being merely cosmetic measures designed to camouflage weak spots. They involve a greater commitment of financial support than we have been willing to make thus far, although we can be optimistic about the chances of some of them being generally accepted and utilized in the future.

5

Interpersonal Relationships

The major factors in teaching the slow learner are the interaction between the child and his teacher and their day-by-day working relationships.

Interpersonal relationships of the teacher and pupil are important for average and bright children, but they are even more crucial for slow learners. Although bright children often learn in spite of the teacher; and the average child can usually weather a rather unsatisfactory year in school, the slow learner is pretty much at the mercy of the school. As stressed earlier, the attitudes and actions of the teacher, whether conscious or unconscious, can have a tremendous impact on the slow learner's ability to profit from his school experiences.

Too often the slow learner has received impersonal treatment. In schools that have self-contained classes, the teachers are often loaded with far too many pupils to do an adequate job of individualizing. On the other hand, in the departmentalized school, the slow learner is apt to be lost in the shuffle; nobody wants to assume the full responsibility for him. He comes in contact with many people, which in itself is not necessarily bad; but the contact is often on a quite impersonal basis. He never develops a real understanding of or respect for any of them. He becomes pretty much a spectator to the educational process of the school. He may spend a period a week with the school counselor, but this is only a very small part of the attention and acceptance he needs.

Modern education is tending to become impersonal. Machines are sometimes used to keep pupils' records and to grade tests. The students even need to carry an ID card to prove they belong in the school. Since our society seems to be drifting in the direction of mechanization, this may be realistic education, relevant to the age; but it is not appropriate for the slow learner. He is not equipped to cope with a highly competitive, impersonal, mechanized world. His special needs must be recognized and dealt with in a deliberate, thoughtful, warm, accepting, and encouraging way.

Our Puritan and Anglo-Saxon heritage tends to compound the problem. It keeps many teachers from allowing themselves the fun of being a warm, loving human being. These individuals are really afraid to get too emotionally involved with their pupils. To give a child a pat on the back, to touch him or to show affection outwardly in any way makes some teachers uncomfortable. They seem to feel that to hold the respect and control of their students they must keep a safe distance. As a result, these teachers miss an important opportunity to reach many deprived and slow learning children when they are most receptive. They let those times when the child's defenses are down and he is most responsive to good influence slip by without taking action.

Of course, carrying this to the extreme and having a gushy, over-indulging, permissive attitude is not wise. The slow learner needs firm control and guidance, sometimes correction; but he accepts and profits from this control better when it comes from a warm, accepting teacher. He usually will accept scolding and criticism without withdrawing if he knows that he will receive recognition and praise when he is good.

Many authorities state that the major hindrance for the borderline mentally retarded child is quite often his own attitude toward himself. His siblings, his friends, and sometimes even his parents have impressed upon him the fact that he is bad and dumb. Then, he may have met with failure at school, which reinforced this belief. Sometimes children will say that their families are ashamed of them. On the other hand, the child's family may be too protective; they may do everything for him because it is easier than having him do it. Thus, he feels very inadequate, even helpless, when faced with a task. Occasionally a teacher will overprotect such a child and help him do things he could very well do for himself.

Until and unless we can undo the damage done by years of neglect or mistreatment and improve the child's self-image, we will have little success in teaching him. We must build his sense of adequacy and his acceptance by others by deliberate and thoughtful means. Here are some of the things we can do to accomplish these ends in the few hours we have him in school.

Getting To Know the Child

First, we must get to know the child, his reactions, his feelings, his special abilities, his interests, and his handicaps. The teacher must utilize every opportunity to visit with the child, encouraging him to talk, drawing him out, leading him on. The teacher who can be a good listener may give the child his first real audience. The better he gets to know the teacher, the greater his trust and the more apt he will be to talk freely.

In these conversations, the child should be told over and over that you have faith in him, that he is not dumb and is able to do the work you give him, that he is good even though he may forget and do naughty things from time to time, and that you are sure he will be a success. You must try to convince him that you are sincerely his friend, that you like him and trust him, and that you recognize his ability. He probably will need this reassurance often, especially at the end of a difficult day. Although this takes time and effort, remember that this is a basic part of *his* readiness period for learning.

The short autobiographical form in the Appendix can be filled out together and will often bring out much hard-to-get information.

Chances for Success

The teacher must insure that the slow learner finds more opportunities for success than for failure. When failure does come, she should help him look upon it with a healthy attitude and a desire to make a greater effort next time. Help him make failure a learning experience. The teacher's attitudes set the tone for the child's.

By failure is meant poor performance in certain tasks, not in general accomplishment. "Failure" is more a state of mind than an actuality and must always be judged in relation to the ability of the child. For example, a slow learner could be praised for a three or four sentence story that has relatively few mistakes, while a bright pupil could be justly criticized for a full page if it contains numerous careless errors. A concerned teacher will make sure that the slow learner will be able to succeed at his work if he tries, because she knows that success tends to bring more success.

Of course, the slow learner should be involved in the ongoing work of the class as much as possible. It is most important for them to feel a part of the group.

Anger and Punishment

When emotional upsets come, do not overreact. Try to redirect the child's thinking or at least allow him a cooling off period before trying to get at the problem. Let him spill out his aggressions, but help direct them into acceptable channels. Keep in mind that when under the stress of anger, the child's language may revert to that of the neighborhood. Most slow learners come from backgrounds where the value systems are not middle class and where the language of anger is often quite colorful. A wise teacher learns to overlook this as much as possible and does not make a great issue of it. If the teacher over-reacts, it will probably cause difficulty later in communications. Always keep in mind that slow learners do not function well in the areas of abstractions and values. They do not understand sarcasm. Keep the discussion of right or wrong on a rather basic level and as concrete as possible.

Should punishment be unavoidable, try to explain the reasons behind it. Assure the child that it is what he did that you dislike, not him as a person. If possible, the punishment should be a learning situation. Try to make it very clear to the child that punishment results when his actions harm himself and those around him. Impress him with the fact that cooperation and self-control bring rewards, but bad conduct can bring punishment. Always make it clear that you will still like him and try to help him.

The type of punishment you use should be based on your knowledge of the child, the school, and the home. Many slow learners may be greatly frightened by being sent to the office. Sometimes, however, this may be the wise thing to do because it removes the child from the room for a short time until things are back to normal and it gives the principal a chance to talk the situation over with the child. Using sarcasm or ridicule or scolding a child in front of his peers is never advisable. One basic rule is to play it cool. An angry teacher is in no condition to make wise judgments about punishment.

Teacher Conferences

In discussing the school work of a slow learner with the pupil or his parents, it is very wise to emphasize progress rather than grade level. Some teachers find that keeping a file of the child's papers gives them a chance to point out growth. In addition, the tape recorder can sometimes be used to show improvement in reading or speech. The teacher should be as encouraging as possible and try to support the child while reassuring the parents.

Time vs. Progress

Some teachers may feel that they are giving their slow learners too much of their time with too little return for their effort. Progress is not as evident with slow learners as it is with brighter pupils. It should be pointed out to these teachers that the small amount of progress made by the slow learner may be far more crucial to his development than the much greater amount made by the bright pupil. The teacher should remember that although the bright student may be influenced by many people, the slow learner may not have anyone who is working to help him but the teacher. Moreover, the slow learner will not progress at all unless special effort is made, but bright and average students will learn with a much smaller proportion of the teacher's time. The help the slow learner receives at school may mean the difference between his becoming a self-supporting citizen or being a ward of society.

It may appear that I am slighting the average or bright pupil, but quite the opposite is true. The suggestions made in this book will benefit all pupils because they tend to create a better climate for learning. Since 1957 and the first Sputnik, our educational system has tended to be overly directed toward the more able student and has overstressed the necessity of a college education for all.

Overprotecting the Slow Learner

Although many of the prior suggestions seem to point in the direction of dependence on the teacher, it must be pointed out that there is nothing to be gained from overprotection. Unquestionably, the slow learner is very dependent upon adults, but an effort should be made to help the slow learner gain confidence so that he will be less dependent. Any measure of independence will come slowly. It will not come from removing your support suddenly. The slow learner will always be less dependent and more inclined to need support and reassurance for a longer period of time than the normal child. The teacher of the slow learner must fight the temptation to do things for him that he could do for himself (with a little help). The slow learner needs encouragement, patience, perseverance, and a friendly push rather than custodial care. Sometimes the teacher may feel that it is easier to do a task herself, but she must resist the urge and remember that her goal for the child is self-confidence and independence.

Overprotectiveness in the relationship of the slow learner with his peers is also unwise. The clever teacher can assist behind the scenes in many ways, but the child must be allowed the opportunity to interact. If he is to become a participating member of the group, he must experience the daily give and take. Obviously, the teacher must stand ready to step in if the situation gets out of hand to prevent real damage to his self-esteem and confidence.

Outlook

The slow learning child, like every other child, is a complex organism. Unlike the normal child, he may have difficulty in overcoming handicaps well enough to get along satisfactorily in school or in society. For this reason, making suggestions that are too specific could be dangerous. The teacher should be cautious about supplying standard remedies before a careful diagnosis is made.

There is good cause for optimism. Much is being learned about learning disabilities and their remedy. If we keep our goals realistic and consider each child as an individual, there is a good chance for success. More materials with which to help the child are becoming available each day.

What is most needed now is for those of us in the classroom to apply what we know wisely. It brings to mind the words of an insolent little sign that one sees quite often: "Don't just stand there! Do something!"

6

Educational Materials for Slow Learners

This chapter contains a listing of available educational materials that have been prepared specifically for slow learners or that have proven to be of value with slow learners. Obviously the listing is not all-inclusive, but a real effort was made to make it reasonably complete. Information about the materials came from personal knowledge of them, from regular classroom teachers or special class teachers who had used them, and from university personnel.

Addresses are listed for most of the entries, but readers are advised to check publishers' catalogs for ordering and pricing information.

Allied Education Council, P. O. Box 78, Galien, Mich. 48113.
- *Fitzhugh Plus Program.* A widely recognized program for teaching language and arithmetic. It uses a problem-oriented approach.
- *Mott Basic Language Skills Program.* An ungraded approach to teaching remedial reading that is useful with slow learners.

American Book Company, 450 W. 33rd St., New York, N.Y. 10001.
- *Dandy Dog's Early Learning Program.* A program designed to stimulate interest in learning to read.
- *The READ System.* A reading program written in a language more natural and lifelike than the traditional reading program. It uses a strong word recognition program based on consistent patterns of sound. Levels 1-6.

American Education Publications, Education Center, Columbus, Ohio 43216.
- *My Weekly Reader,* Levels K-6. One of the best-known student newspapers, long used with benefit in teaching slow learners.
- *Paperback Book Club.* A source of fine, inexpensive paperbacks at all reading levels.
- *Pictorial Aids.* Beautiful sets of pictures in full color. Weekly Reader Science Photos, 8 sets with 8 photos each.
- *Practice Books.* (For use in middle grades and junior high.) Read-Study-Think Booklets, Science Reading Adventures, Imagine and Write.
- *The Triple I Series* (Ideas, Images, and I). This series, which is available in either paperback or hardbound books, is designed to help the student develop healthy attitudes toward himself, his family, his friends, his school, and his community. Levels 1-6. Useful in compensatory programs.

American Guidance Service, Inc., Publisher's Building, Circle Pines, Minn. 55014.
- *First Grade Screening Test* (Pate and Webb). Group test used at end of kindergarten or the start of first grade to identify children with potential learning problems. The test was designed to identify three major types of handicaps: intellectual deficiency, central nervous system dysfunction, or emotional disturbances. Separate booklets for boys and girls.
- *Peabody Language Development Kits.* Four levels. (Dunn, Smith, and Horton). Four self-centered kits of lessons and materials designed to stimulate cognitive functioning and achievement through oral language development. These are excellent, highly-motivating materials useful for the slow learner and other pupils who have difficulty with verbal expression and conceptualization.

- *Peabody Rebus Reading Program.* An excellent programmed workbook course at primary levels using rebuses rather than spelling words. Transition is made to regular words and word analysis through phonics.

Behavioral Research Laboratories, 866 United Nations Plaza, New York, N.Y. 10017.

- *Project Read.* A comprehensive selection of materials designed to upgrade reading. Uses a linguistic decoding approach in a programmed format. This series is based on the research of Dr. M. W. Sullivan.

Benefic Press, 10300 W. Roosevelt Rd., Westchester, Ill. 60153.
Publishes a variety of materials suitable for use with slow learners. The materials are excellent and have a great appeal to the reluctant reader. Since all of the books are written on an interest level that is much above the listed reading level, they are widely applicable in the elementary grades. Teachers manuals are available for many.

- *Animal Adventure Books* (with records, 10 books). Preprimer to grade 1.
- *Butternut Bill Series* (7 books). Preprimer to grade 1.
- *Cowboy Sam Series* (19 books). Preprimer to grade 3.
- *Cowboys of Many Lands* (4 books). Grades K-6.
- *Don Frontier Series* (with records, 11 books). Preprimer to grade 4.
- *Moonbeam Series* (9 books). Preprimer to grade 3.
- *Mystery Adventure Series* (8 books). Grades 2-6.
- *Sailor Jack Series* (10 books). Preprimer to grade 5.
- *Space Age Books* (8 books). Grades 1-3.
- *Space Science Fiction* (6 books). Grades 2-6.
- *Sports Mystery Series* (4 books). Grades 2-3.
- *Tom Logan Series* (7 books). Preprimer to grade 3.
- *World Adventure Series* (8 books). Grades 2-6.

Bell & Howell (Purchase through local distributor).

- *Language Master.* An audiovisual instructional device with worthwhile applications for the slow learner or learning disabled child. Utilizes printed picture cards with a sound track. Card sets are available at all grade levels in language arts.
- *House of Books.* Kits of materials at grades 1-3 suitable for use by remedial or slow readers.

- *Oral Reading and Linguistic Series.* Grades 1-6. These books have dramatic literary content. The exercises are designed to improve speech patterns and linguistic skills. This series is unusual because of the emphasis on oral reading.

BIPAD, 122 E. 42nd St., New York, N.Y. 10017.
- *The Paperback Goes to School.* This helpful listing was compiled by committees of N.E.A., Association of School Librarians, and N.C.T.E. Lists over 4,500 current paperbacks suitable for school use by subject and title.

The Bobbs-Merrill Co., Inc., 4300 W. 62nd St., Indianapolis, Ind. 96206.
Publishes a good developmental reading program of text-workbooks. Levels from preprimer through grade 6. This inexpensive program is a good way to provide a variety of ability levels for pupils in a classroom. Teachers' annotated editions, which contain 3 tests at each level, are available.

Stanley Bowmar Co., Inc., Valhalla, N.Y. 10595.
- *Multimedia Reading Incentive Program.* A highly motivating series of books, filmstrips, and records starting at third grade level with such titles as *Teen Fair, Surfing,* and *Motorcycles.* Designed to appeal to boys particularly. The content and reading level makes these materials suitable for slow learners in the intermediate grades through high school.

Chicago Archdiocesan Reading Service, 126 W. Desplaines St., Chicago, Ill. 60606.
- *A Handbook of Information on the Delacato Neurological Approach.* A helpful booklet for those who wish to learn more about this approach to learning problems.

Childrens Press, 1224 W. Van Buren St., Chicago, Ill. 60607.
- *I Want To Be Books* (36 books). Easy-to-read books about occupations and professions.
- *The True Books* (60 books). Popular series of easy-to-read, well-illustrated factual books with science and social studies content. Adaptable to different reading levels.

The Continental Press, Inc., Elizabethtown, Pa. 17022.
A source of inexpensive but good quality printed or spirit duplicating

teaching materials at all levels and in a number of subjects. Widely used in many schools.

Dell Publishing Co., Inc., 750 Third Ave., New York, N.Y. 10017.
* *Yearling Books.* A series of top quality paperbacks, many of which are award winners. A good source of books for the poor reader in junior or senior high school.

T. S. Denison & Co., Inc., 5100 W. 82nd St., Minneapolis, Minn. 55431.
Four useful books of practical suggestions for accommodating the mentally retarded child in the classroom, by Janet K. Thomas. Many of the ideas are applicable to the slow learner.
* Book 1 — *Teaching and Administering Classes for Mentally Retarded Children.*
* Book 2 — *Teaching Arithmetic to Mentally Retarded Children.*
* Book 3 — *Teaching Language Arts to Mentally Retarded Children.*
* Book 4 — *Teaching Reading to Mentally Retarded Children.*

Developmental Learning Materials, 3505 N. Ashland Ave., Chicago, Ill. 60657.
Specializes in learning materials for the young learning disabled child, especially those with brain damage. Many of the items would be of value to the slow learning child in kindergarten and the primary grades.

Doubleday & Company, Inc., 277 Park Ave., New York, N.Y. 10017.
Specialized books, tapes, and records that are designed to help the slow reader make the transition from prereading experiences to independent reading.

Ealing Film Loops, 2225 Massachusetts Ave., Cambridge, Mass. 02140.
One of the larger suppliers of easy-to-use cartridge film loops. Cost ranges from $19.50 to $21.50 per film. Can be projected for a whole class or for individual or small groups using an inexpensive daylight viewer. Their largest list of subjects includes the Disney nature films.

The Economy Company, 1901 N. Walnut Ave., Oklahoma City, Okla. 73105.
A good source of text-workbooks and materials for use in building phonics and reading skills. These have been used extensively for regular classwork and for individualized programs.

Educational Development Laboratories, Huntington, N.Y. 11744.
Materials that utilize a controlled speed filmstrip flasher that can be
used to develop coordination, mobility, and quicker response. Filmstrips are available in special reading programs, spelling and arithmetic
skills.

Educational Reading Service, Inc., East 64 Midland Ave., Paramus,
N.J. 07652.

• *Paperback Classroom Library.* Inexpensive, high quality paperbacks. Hundreds of titles from kindergarten level and up. They may
  be purchased separately or in collections.

Electronics Futures, Inc., 57 Dodge Ave., North Haven, Conn. 46473.
Specializes in audiovisual materials and equipment for teaching reading, math, science, and literature. Uses cassette tapes and accompanying printed materials. The teacher who has the equipment for this
type of teaching should investigate these materials for use with slow
learners.

Fearon Publishers, Lear Siegler, Inc., Education Division, 6 Davis
Dr., Belmont, Calif. 94002.
Pacemaker Books is the imprint for a line of readers and text-
workbooks for slow learners, the educable mentally retarded, and
reluctant readers. These books provide high interest material at a
very low reading ability level. Free teacher's manuals with most
Pacemaker Books.

• *Pacemaker Story Books.* A series of 24 books written especially for
  the educable mentally retarded and slow learners. High interest level
  with reading levels from 1.9 to 2.6.
      Set 1:
      Around the Town: Three Short Stories (Crosher).
      Island Adventure (Crosher).
      Mystery Cottage (Crosher).
      The Strange Artist (Crosher).
      Trail to Adventure (Crosher).
      Uncle Bill Comes Home (Crosher).
      Set 2:
      Adventure in the Snow (Crosher).
      A Bomb in the Submarine (Crosher).
      A Gun from Nowhere (Crosher).

Mystery at Camp Sunshine (Crosher).
Ride on a Rainy Afternoon (Crosher).
Treasure in the Ruins (Crosher).
Set 3:
Catch Tom Rudd! (Crosher).
The Clubhouse Mystery (Silsbee).
The Fire on the First Floor (Crosher).
The Haunted House (Crosher).
The Man Without a Memory (Crosher).
Over the Rickety Fence (Battles).
Set 4:
Around Home: Three Short Stories (Crosher).
By the Sea: Three Short Stories (Crosher).
Devil's Rock (Crosher).
Night Adventure (Crosher).
Robbery at Blair's (Crosher).
Trouble on the Farm (Crosher).

- *Pacemaker Classics.* Abridged and adapted versions that retain the flavor and excitement of the original. Teen-aged interest level, second grade reading level.
  The Jungle Book (Kipling).
  The Last of the Mohicans (Cooper).
  The Moonstone (Collins).
  Robinson Crusoe (Defoe).
  Treasure Island (Stevenson).
  Two Years Before the Mast (Dana).

- *Pacemaker True Adventures.* Informative and enjoyable books. Each book contains 3 true stories describing important moments in the lives of notable men and women. Reading levels 2.0 to 2.5.
  Tales of Animals (Jerrome).
  Tales of Escape (Jerrome).
  Tales of Flying (Jerrome).
  Tales of Shipwreck (Jerrome).

- *Adventures in Space.* A continuous story within each set of 3 books and within the whole series. But each book contains a complete story in itself and does not require previous reading for comprehension. No teacher's manual. Reading levels 2.5 through 3.5.
  Moonflight (McCullagh), 3 books.

Journey to Mars (McCullagh), 3 books.

Red Planet (McCullagh), 3 books.

Journey to a New Earth (McCullagh), 3 books.

- *Eddie in School* (Piltch). Thirty one-page stories about a teen-age city boy to help students learn how and why things are done in school, at home, at work, and in the community. Includes comprehension and word skill exercises. Reading level 2.2.
- *Getting a Job* (Randall). This illustrated text-workbook is a realistic presentation of what kinds of jobs there are and how to read and use help wanted ads, make applications, go for interviews, and fill out forms. Reading level 3.6.
- *I Can Draw* (Dickey). Contains enjoyable cartoon figures that can be copied or traced to help students learn the art of cartooning. No teacher's manual.
- *Jerry Works in a Service Station* (Wade). First in a series of vocational text-workbooks. Contains much practical information on how to get a job and the duties of a service station worker as well as exercises on vocational content and language arts skills. Reading level 2.2.
- *Measure Up* (Kahn, Herring, and Tong). Introduces students to linear measurement and helps them learn how to measure. Reading level 2.7.
- *Money Makes Sense* (Kahn and Hanna). This text-workbook can be used to help teach arithmetic by the use of money problems. Very practical material for slow learners. Reading level 2.8.
- *Using Dollars and Sense* (Kahn and Hanna). More advanced content involving use of money. Reading level about 3.6.
- *Planning Meals and Shopping* (Weaver). First in the new "Young Homemakers at Work" series. Designed to help both male and female students learn to perform two basic homemaking tasks effectively. Reading level 2.5.
- *Plans for Living: Your Guide to Health and Safety* (Hudson and Weaver). This text-workbook is a practical personal guide for the development of the student's physical and emotional well-being. Reading level 2.8.
- *Time and Telling Time* (Wiley). Sequenced somewhat like a programmed book, this text-workbook will motivate the student in mastering the task of telling time. Reading level 2.9.

- *To Be a Good American* (Weaver). A series of 4 text-workbooks designed to develop the student's potential for good citizenship. Reading levels 3.3 to 3.9.
    Book 1—*In Your Family.*
    Book 2—*In Your Community.*
    Book 3—*In Your State.*
    Book 4—*In Your Country.*
- *You and Your World* (Bolinger). This social studies text-workbook was designed to help the slow learner understand more about himself, his family, school, neighborhood, city, county, state, country and the world. Uses easy vocabulary (Grade 2.3) and contains a variety of interesting projects and activities.

Fearon Teacher-Aid Books, another line of this publisher, contain many proven devices for stimulating learning. Some representative books are:
- *Arithmetic Games* (Dumas).
- *How To Meet Individual Differences in Teaching Arithmetic* (Dumas, Kittel, and Grant).
- *Phonics Handbook for the Primary Grades* (Mellin).
- *Teach Spelling by All Means* (Clanfield and Hannan).

Field Educational Publications, Inc., 609 Mission St., San Francisco, Calif. 94105.
- *Americans All Series.* A series about Americans of varying racial and ethnic backgrounds. Useful with older slow learners. Reading level 4.4.
- *The Checkered Flag Series.* Eight books of high interest to older slow learners who like cars, motorcycles, racing, etc. Reading levels from 2.4 to 4.5.
- *Corrective Reading Programs* (formerly Harr-Wagner series). Widely used high interest, low vocabulary books. Format and content will appeal to most reluctant and poor readers. Good literary quality and content in natural science, oceanography, and conservation.
- *Series with controlled reading levels from 1.7 to 2.2.*
    Jim Forest Readers (4 books).
    Deep Sea Adventures (2 books).
    Morgan Bay Mysteries (7 books).

- *Reading Levels 2.6 to 3.2.*
    Jim Forest Readers (4 books).
    Deep Sea Adventures (2 books).
    Morgan Bay Mysteries (7 books).
- *Reading Levels 3.5 to 5.0.*
    Deep Sea Adventures (3 books).
    Morgan Bay Mysteries (5 books).
    Wildlife Adventures (4 books).
- *Time Machine Series.* Exciting science fiction with historical content. Reading level up to 2.5.

Follett Educational Corp., 1010 W. Washington Blvd., Chicago, Ill. 60607.
- *The Frostig Developmental Program.* Useful for preparing children for exercises in reading, writing, arithmetic, and other academic work.
- *The Frostig Picture and Pattern Material.* Three sequential picture and pattern books to be used in kindergarten to second grade.
- *Tests for detecting children with learning problems.*
    Early Detection Inventory (McGahan). Preschool and primary age.
    Developmental Test of Visual-Motor Integration (Berz-Buktenica). Preschool through grade 3.
    Evanston Early Identification Scale (Laudsmann-Dillard). Five years through 6 years, 3 months.

Follett Publishing Company, 201 N. Wells St., Chicago, Ill. 60606.
- *Adventure in Nature and Science.* Thirteen books that are illustrated with full-color photographs. Can be used from grade 3 on.
- *American History Study Lessons* (Abramowitz). Content for high school and young adults. Reading level at about sixth grade.
- *Boxcar Children Mysteries* (Warner). This series of 13 books is one of the pioneer efforts at high interest, low vocabulary books for poor readers.
- *Frontier of America books* (McCall). Twenty well-written books on American history for slow readers.
- *Learning Your Language,* Books I and II. A language arts program for use with junior high or high school pupils. Reading level begins at about 3.5 and progresses to about grade 6.

- *Let's Travel Books*. Twenty-three geographical readers, with easy-to-read text and full-color photographs.
- *Spache materials*. Dr. Spache has prepared a number of fine publications that help to relate school materials to the reading ability of the pupil.
- *Study Lessons in Civics* (Ball and Rosch). Designed to help older disabled readers develop an understanding of government and their role as citizens.
- *Study Lessons in General Science* (Gross and Kipilow). Content suitable for junior and senior high school students. About fifth grade reading level.
- *Study Lessons in Our Nation's History* (Abramowitz). Eight units of American history suitable for use with older slow learners. Reading level starts at fourth grade and advances to about seventh grade.
- *Success in Language and Literature* (Tincher et al.). Levels A, B, and C. This language arts program was especially written for slow learners and other children who have reading problems. It reflects the everyday problems of teen-age youth in an urban setting. Grades 5-6.
- *The Tizz Books*. Thirteen exciting, easy-to-read horse stories with social studies content. Wide interest range; could be used at reading levels from upper primary on.
- *Turner Career Guidance Series*. These books for high school slow learners discuss vital information relative to the working world.
- *Turner-Livingston Communications Series*. Six volumes including such titles as *Television You Watch* or *Movies You See*. Teen-age interest level, but fourth to fifth grade reading level.
- *Turner-Livingston Reading Series*. Six volumes for use with older pupils who have a reading problem. The content relates well to youth and their everyday problems.
- *Vocational Reading Series*. Six volumes. An excellent series designed to develop reading and comprehension skills while giving useful information about common vocations. Teen-age interest level and fifth grade reading level.
- *World History Study Lessons* (Abramowitz). Materials similar to those in American history.

Garrard Publishing Co., 1607 N. Market St., Champaign, Ill. 61820.

- *Basic Vocabulary Books.* This series uses the Dolch list of 220 basic words plus 95 of the commonest nouns. Interest level up to sixth grade; reading level, grade 2. There are 7 books of true animal stories, 4 of folklore, and 5 of Indian folklore.
- *Discovery* (ed. Austin). A set of 55 fast-moving biographical stories filled with excitement and historical information. These excellent books for slow readers are well-illustrated and have a reading level about 3.0. Almost all children love biographies, and these are ideal for the disabled reader.
- *The Dolch 220 Basic Sight Vocabulary.* These materials are based on the Dolch study showing that the 220 words on the list comprise about 65% of the words in first and second readers and 50% of the words in all other school books. The materials are widely used in many ways. The set can be purchased in the form of flash cards for individual or group use, or in the form of games.
- *Folklore of the World Series.* An appealing set of stories that gives slow learners a glimpse of the customs and culture of people around the world. A simple reading vocabulary under 700 words is used, and the reading level is about grade 3. These books will prove popular with slow learners in grades 4-8, or even higher.
- *Junior Science Books* (ed. Larrick). Approximately 25 books about natural science. Highly rated series of good high interest, low reading level books.
- *Pleasure Reading Books.* A set of 13 retold classics in a form that will appeal to slow readers. Reading level is about fourth grade; interest level is junior high and above.

Ginn and Company, Statler Bldg., Back Bay P.O. 191, Boston, Mass. 02117.

- *The Ginn Basic Reading Program.* Although not primarily designed for slow learners, the overall excellence of this reading program makes it useful when additional materials for individualizing are needed. The third, fourth, fifth, and sixth grade readers could all be used at higher grade levels without losing their appeal. Teacher's manuals and teacher's editions of this series are outstanding and contain a wealth of suggestions for accommodating the handicapped or reluctant reader.

Globe Book Company, Inc., 175 Fifth Ave., New York, N.Y. 10010. Has a great many publications prepared especially for the slow learner. Some of these touch areas in the curriculum not ordinarily covered by such materials.

- *Adapted Classics.* A group of 47 great books adapted for the slow learner. Reading levels 4-8.
- *Afro-American in the United States* (DeSilva, Finklestein, and Loshins).
- *American Folklore and Legends* and *Myths and Folk Tales Around the World.* Two action-filled books for slow or reluctant readers in junior or senior high. Reading level is grade 4.
- *Exploring American History* (Schwartz and O'Connor).
- *Exploring Our Nation's History* (Schwartz and O'Connor).
- *Exploring World History* (Holt and O'Connor). Four history texts written with controlled vocabulary, simple sentence structure, and short chapters. Exercises are included on the essential concepts.
- *Great Adventures, Great Americans,* and *Great Lives* (Low). Three books of adventure stories and biographies with sixth grade reading level.
- *Pathways in Science.* A complete science program prepared for slow learners. A total of 12 books—3 in biology, 3 in earth science, 3 in chemistry, and 3 in physics. Reading levels 5-6. Available in paperback or clothbound.
- *Real Stories,* Books 1 and 2. (Katz, Chakeres, and Bromberg). Readers especially written for older slow learners. Reading levels 4.5 to 5. A skills program is included for remedial use.
- *Stories for Teen-agers.* Collections of current writings of interest to teen-agers. Good for the junior or senior high slow learner.

Golden Press, 850 Third Ave., New York, N.Y. 10022.
- *Golden Encyclopedia.* The set is profusely illustrated and easy to read. It can be used by slow learners in junior high who might be unable to read standard encyclopedias. The reading level is about grade 4.

Harcourt Brace Jovanovich, Inc., 757 Third Ave., New York, N.Y. 10017.
- *The Bookrack Reading Program.* A new series of linguistic readers at levels of 1-6.

- *Palo Alto Reading Program: Sequential Steps in Reading.* A comprehensive primary reading program for nongraded use. Based on the sound-symbol relationship in language. An eclectic program containing features of various successful reading methods. Widely adaptable. Grades 1-3.

Harper & Row, Publishers, 49 E. 33rd St., New York, N.Y. 10016.

- *The American Adventures Stories* (ed. Betts). This group of 22 books has been expertly written to motivate slow readers. There are five vocabulary levels from grades 2 to 6. The stories are about famous Americans and are especially interesting to boys. Teacher's guides available for each book.
- *Basic Science Education Series* (Parker, Blough, O'Donnell). This wonderful series of paperback booklets is ideal for use with slow learners. The material is authentic and well-illustrated. Each Unitext is 36 pages long. Reading levels range from grade 1 through junior high.
- *Torchbearer Libraries I and II.*
    I—37 books, reading level 3-5.
    II—34 books, reading level 4-6.
- *Torchlighter Libraries I and II.*
    I—44 books, reading level 3-5.
    II—36 books, reading level 2-4.

Hoffman Information System, 5623 Peek Rd., Arcadia, Calif. 91006. Offers quite a lot of audiovisual materials that can be used to teach reading, oral language, spelling, and writing. Usable with most new reading series.

Holt, Rinehart & Winston, Inc., 383 Madison Ave., New York, N.Y. 10017.

- *Instant Reader.* This series is designed to help every child read independently almost immediately. Grades 1-3.
- *I Wonder Why Readers.* Exciting reading material on scientific subjects. Twenty-four books with full-color illustrations.
- *Owl Books* (ed. Martin). A delightful collection of beautifully illustrated books that help children develop insight into ever-expanding horizons. Many topics are covered. Slow learners enjoy these bright, easy-to-read books.
    20 *Kin/der Owls* (K-1).

40 *Little Owls* (1-2).
40 *Young Owls* (2-4).
20 *Wise Owls* (4-6).

- *Sounds and Patterns of Language* (Martin, Weil, and Kohan). A complete kit of materials in a life-related sequential program to develop reading readiness through facility with language. Designed for language disadvantaged children at preschool, primary level. Contains many kinds of teaching material.
- *Sounds of Language Readers.* Linguistic readers in which reading represents a total language experience.

Houghton Mifflin Company, 2 Park St., Boston, Mass. 02107.

- *Paper Books.* Fine biographical books for use with slow learners in grades 6-8.
- *Reading Skills Labs* (Dure and Hillauch). Materials for diagnosing and correcting reading disabilities in older pupils beyond grade 4. An individualized approach with no grade level markings on books.

Imperial International Learning, Box 548, Kankakee, Ill. 60901.
One of the largest producers of educational reel-to-reel or cassette tapes, most of which would find application in reinforcement teaching of slow learners. There is a comprehensive listing by grade and subject. One of their series is the *St. Louis Programs,* which are an individualized approach to speech improvement and reading readiness for grades 1-3. They also offer inexpensive, good quality tape players.

Kimbo Records, Box 55, Deal, N.J. 07723.
An excellent source for records to assist in physical coordination exercises and rhythmic games.

Knowledge Aids, Division of Radiant Corp., 8220 N. Austin Ave., Morton Grove, Ill. 60053.

- *Follow Through with Sounds.* A well-planned set of materials to assist in the development of auditory perception skills. Consists of teachers' guides, a set of full-color transparencies, full-color study prints, and sound recordings on cartridges, tapes, or LP records.

Lerner Publications Co., 241 First Ave. N., Minneapolis, Minn. 55401.

- *Mr. Bumba Books.* A series of easy readers of fanciful stories that children love.

- *Mrs. Moon Books.* A series about an elderly, retired librarian and her little friends. Good reading for reluctant or handicapped readers.
- *Pull Ahead Books.* A series of books with a fourth grade reading level and sixth to eleventh grade interest level. For boys and girls.

J. B. Lippincott Co., E. Washington Sq., Philadelphia, Pa. 19105.

- *Glim and Manchester Basic Keys in Spelling.* This series has the same phonics, linguistic approach as the basic reading series. Useful for slow learners who need an extra phonics program.
- *McCracken and Walcutt Basic Reading Series.* A new edition of Lippincott's phonics, linguistic basal readers. The series includes a wealth of supplemental material at every grade level. Available in regular or multi-ethnic editions.

Lyons and Carnahan, 407 E. 25th St., Chicago, Ill. 60616.

- *Motivation Readers.* Six readers that have a highly motivating content and appeal. Suitable for nongraded use. Teacher's edition available for each reader.

    The Blue Dog and Other Stories (1st level).
    The Flying Squirrel and Other Stories (2nd level).
    The Almost Ghost and Other Stories (3rd level).
    The Barking Cat and Other Stories (4th level).
    Better than Gold and Other Stories (5th level).
    Three Green Men and Other Stories (6th level).

- *Phonics We Learn Game Kit.* A kit of 10 games that help in developing phonics skill.
- *Spelling Learning Games Kit.* A set of 5 games designed to teach spelling skills.
- *Young America Basic Reading Program.* A new reading program that requires the child to reach conclusions independently. Kindergarten-grade 8.

McGraw-Hill Book Co. (Webster Division), Manchester Rd., Manchester, Mo. 63011.

Publishes several collections of low reading level, high interest books.

- *Classic Fairy Tales* (9 books). Reading level 2.8.
- *Corkey, Kim, and Hickory Books* (10 books). Reading level 1.9.
- *The Everyreader Series* (21 paperbacks). Famous literary works rewritten on a high interest, low reading level (fourth grade or below).

- *Read for Fun Series* (10 books). Interest level ages 7-10.
- *Skyline Series* (4 books). Written for disadvantaged urban pupils. Reading levels range from 1.4 to 3.3.
- *Story Shelf I* (25 books). Primary books chosen by Dr. George Spache.
- *Sullivan Storybooks* (35 books). Reading levels are grades 1 to 3.
- *Programmed Reading.* An individualized program that can be used as basal in the primary grades and corrective in the middle grades. The programmed format allows children to work independently. Available at a number of reading levels.

Charles E. Merrill Publishing Co., 1300 Alum Creek Dr., Columbus, Ohio 43216.

- *Diagnostic Reading Workbook Series.* A series of inexpensive reading workbooks designed to be used for extra drill during the year, or for summer "refresher." Contains standardized diagnostic tests. Levels 1 through 6.
- *Merrill Mainstream Books.* A series of five paperback anthologies of works by outstanding writers directed toward acquainting the disadvantaged with the mainstream of American social and educational life. Prepared especially for the slow learner or reluctant reader of junior and senior high age with reading levels of grades 4 to 7.5.
- *New Phonics Skill-text Series.* A series of ungraded work-texts that are designed to provide much-needed drill on the phonetic skills useful in reading and spelling. Can be used with slow learners from grades 2-8. When used with the accompanying Skill-tapes, they could be of considerable value.
- *New Reading Skill-text Series.* An attractive series of work-text readers that have their own standardized tests. Although graded 1-6, they could be used on a nongraded basis at higher levels. Skill-tapes are available for each reader, a useful feature if your pupils need added reinforcement. This series is inexpensive enough to make it available to all schools for individualizing.
- *Phonics Skill-texts and Tapes.* Excellent for individualizing remedial work. Primary and intermediate; can be used with slow learners at higher levels. Stresses word sounds, structure, and understanding.

Millikin Publishing Co., 611 Olive St., St. Louis, Mo. 63101.

Publishes many unusual and inexpensive materials that are relevant to programs for slow learners. Many of the materials are workbooks in which the original spirit master is also a transparency. Some include a record or tape and teacher's guide.

National Wildlife Federation, 1412 16th St., N.W., Washington, D.C. 20036.

- *Ranger Rick's Nature Magazine.* This beautiful and exciting new nature magazine is excellent for use with intermediate, junior high, or even high school slow readers. Can be obtained at a group rate of $5 per year. Every classroom should have it.

New York Times Teaching Resources Div., 100 Boylston St., Boston, Mass. 02116.

- *Dubinoff School Program.* One level, "Experiential Perceptual-motor Exercises."

Noble & Noble Publishers, Inc., 750 Third Ave., New York, N.Y. 10017.

- *Chandler Reading Series.* A reading program that has a multi-ethnic approach and is "boy" oriented, which makes it particularly useful. Stories utilize a real-life approach and are directed toward helping the child identify and build a positive self-image.
- *Crossroads Series.* Five paperback readers of junior and senior high interest and low reading ability.
- *Falcon Books Series.* Abridged editions of best sellers, paperbacks. Teacher's notes available.
- *TRY—Exercises for Young Children.* A carefully prepared set of visual-perceptual materials for children aged 4-7. The material was planned to present experiences that develop visual-motor skills, speaking, thinking, and listening skills, oral and physical self expression, and a positive self-image.

Norelco (Buy through distributor.)

- *Norelco FM Wireless Learning System.* This auditory input system provides an FM transmitter and individual receiver headphones for individual or group listening. Can be used in libraries, cafeterias, auditoriums, study halls, or classrooms without the necessity of wiring each listening unit. Any audio device can be used—cassette or reel-to-reel recorder, radio, phonograph, or microphone. The student can listen without disturbing or being disturbed by others. This offers a benefit to slow learners who need a repetition or review of materials or special teaching tapes. The children may sit at their own desks and do not have to be grouped around a table.

Open Court Publishing Co., 1039 Eighth St., La Salle, Ill. 61301.
This series has attracted an unusual amount of attention, and schools using it report excellent results.
- *Open Court Reading Series.* For older pupils (grade 4 and above) who have failed to acquire a good foundation for independent reading. High interest stories are used. This is primarily a phonics approach.

George A. Pflaum, Publisher, 38 W. Fifth St., Dayton, Ohio 45402.
- *Dimensions of Personality Series.* These books, which can be used in middle grades and higher, are useful in helping a child understand himself and in building self-respect.
  Book 4—*Here I Am.*
  Book 5—*I'm Not Alone.*
  Book 6—*Becoming Myself.*

G. P. Putman's Sons, 200 Madison Ave., New York, N.Y. 10016.
Offers hundreds of fine, high-quality, easy-to-read books. It is an excellent source of books for the slow learner to use in reading, literature, social studies, and science. Books are written by such famous writers for children as Raymond Briggs, Hardie Gramatky, Syd Hoff, Jean Fritz, and many others.
- *Let's Go Books.* Primary.
- *See and Read Books.* Primary.
- *Building America Series.* Intermediate.
- *Getting To Know Books.* Intermediate.

Random House, Inc., 201 E. 50th St., New York, N.Y. 10022.
- *Reading Pacesetters.* Five kits of materials designed for individualized instruction in reading. Each kit consists of 50 carefully selected books from Random House, Knopf, and Pantheon. Useful for slow learners in the middle grades or junior to senior high.

Raytheon Education Company, 285 Columbus Ave., Boston, Mass. 02116.
- *Miami Linguistic Readers.* A special series of beginning readers for use with those pupils who do not speak acceptable oral English or who are learning to speak and read English.

- *Teen-age Tales* (Strang). Collections of short stories and articles written for the older pupil with a reading handicap. The 9 books in the series have reading levels from grade 3 to grade 6. Usable in junior high and secondary school.

Reader's Digest Association, Pleasantville, N.Y. 10570.
- *Reader's Digest Skill Builders.* Outstanding workbooks for use with slow learners and reluctant readers. Printed in regular *Reader's Digest* format. Levels from 1-8, all with carefully controlled vocabulary. Practice pads are available if desired. Has teachers editions:

four at level 1	six at level 5
four at level 1 +	six at level 6
five at level 2	two at level 7
six at level 3	two at level 8
six at level 4	

Scholastic Book Services, Div. of Scholastic Magazines, Inc., 50 W. 44th St., New York, N.Y. 10036.
- *Reader's Choice.* An excellent source of high-quality paperbacks of all types and reading levels. Prices are unusually low.
- *Let's Find Out Materials.* Preprimary or kindergarten. The *Weekly Reader* is an improvement over the ordinary school newspaper because it contains colorful, multisensory materials. It can be used on a nongraded basis. Standardized diagnostic tests plus a teacher's magazine are included.

News Pilot—grade 1.
News Ranger—grade 2.
News Trails—grade 3.
News Explorer—grade 4.
Young Citizen—grade 5.
Newstime, Jr. Scholastic—grade 6.

Science Research Associates, Inc., 259 E. Erie St., Chicago, Ill. 60611.
- *The DISTAR Program.* One of the better new remedial programs for preschool and primary children. Although it can be used to teach reading, language, and arithmetic to all children, it is especially useful with disadvantaged children or slow learners. Planned by Dr. Siegfried Englemann, it assumes that every child can learn if properly taught. The program has proven to be very successful.

- *Newsletter Series for Teachers.* Sets of 20 informative and scholarly bulletins of value to the teacher of the slow learner. Four of the sets are:

  Communications Skills for the Disadvantaged Learner (Ducchioni).

  The Nongraded School (Dawson).

  Team Teaching (Troutt).

  Nuts and Bolts of Elementary Education (Davis and Christian).

Scott, Foresman and Company, 1900 E. Lake Ave., Glenview, Ill. 60025.

- *Adapted Classics.* A series of famous novels adapted for older children with low reading ability. They have been made easy to read without destroying their quality or style.
- *Easy Reading Books.* This series of 18 books has a real appeal to the slow learner or reluctant reader in the middle or upper grades. Students will really enjoy these superior quality action stories.
- *Multisensory Teaching Aids.* A wide range of aids that will assist the slow learner in overcoming particular difficulties. These can be used with any reading program.
- *Open Highway Series.* An excellent set of basal readers with accompanying workbooks, transparencies, and seatwork. Especially written for the disadvantaged reader.

Silver Burdett Company, 250 James St., Morristown, N.J. 07960.

- *Silver Burdett Picture Packets.* Three series of 19″ x 23″ full-color photographs. These are so outstanding that they can be used in many ways and at different grade levels to start children talking and to bring out concepts and information. They really prove the old adage that one picture is worth a thousand words. Although the content is primarily social studies, for the slow learner they would be applicable to a wide range of subjects.

  Famous Around-the-World Holidays and Special Occasions.

  The Earth, Home of People.

  Families Around the World.

- *Young Reader's Edition of the Life Nature Library.* Special editions of the famous Time-Life books that have been written for slow readers. A fine source of science and social studies material for the slow learner.

Singer School Division, Random House, Inc., 201 E. 50th St., New York, N.Y. 10022.

- *The Carousel Book Program.* Seven carefully selected, well-balanced book collections for individualized reading in all of the primary grades.
- *Drill and Practice Kits for Individualizing Mathematics* (Suppes and Jerman). A kit of materials to improve computational skills through an individualized approach. Primarily for grades 3 to 6, but could be used with slow learners at the junior high level.
- *Experiencing Mathematics.* A work-text program designed for remedial use at the junior high level. Progresses from Book A, which starts at a third grade level, to Book E, which reaches a general senior math level.
- *Structural Reading Program.* These paperback text-workbooks use a modified linguistic and decoding approach. The program is flexible and allows an individualized rate of progress. The authors prepared these materials with the idea that no school child needs to experience failure in learning to read. For grades 1 and 2.

Society for Visual Education, Inc., 1345 Diversey Pkwy., Chicago, Ill. 60614.

Seven sets of great value in science instruction for the slow learner. Each set contains 20 color slides and a descriptive guide for the teacher's use. Excellent teaching materials at any level. Children enjoy seeing them over and over.

> *Common Zoo Animals.*
> *Common Pets.*
> *Common Farm and Ranch Animals.*
> *Common Birds That Live Near People.*
> *Common Birds of the Woodland.*
> *Common Insects and Spiders.*
> *Common Butterflies and Moths.*

Steck-Vaughn Company, Box 2028, Austin, Tex. 78767.

- *Imaginary Line Handwriting Materials.* This set of books and related materials, including special practice pads, offers more than the usual help to the slow learner in proper letter formation and in forming accurate images of letters and words. He learns where to start and stop, height, size, and shape.

Teachers College Press, Columbia University, 1234 Amsterdam Ave., New York, N.Y. 10027.
- *Perceptual Training Activities Handbook* (Van Witsen). An inexpensive paperback filled with ideas for activities for training and correcting children with perceptual handicaps.

Teachers Publishing Corp., 22 W. Putnam Ave., Greenwich, Conn. 06830.
- *Individualized Phonics Program.* This is one of the better programs in phonics in that it is more flexible and comprehensive. The material is presented so that each student progresses at his own rate. Six levels, 8 books.

Wollensak Teaching Tapes (Available through distributors of audio-visual materials such as Selected Educational Aids, Inc., Evanston, Ill. 60201.)
A source for either reel-to-reel or cassette teaching tapes. These are available from kindergarten level up and include many that would fit a program for teaching the slow learner.

Zaner-Bloser Co., 612 N. Park St., Columbus, Ohio 43215.
- *New Correlated Handwriting Filmstrips.* Set of 4 covering both capital and lowercase letters in manuscript and cursive..
- *New Handwriting Filmstrips.* Two color filmstrips useful with slow learners in the middle or upper grades who have difficulty with letters and letter formation (cursive).
- *Peek Thru Plastic Alphabet Guides.* For either manuscript or cursive. Inexpensive enough that each pupil can have one to use to compare letter formation by placing the model over his own. A very helpful device.

Appendix

The autobiographical form entitled "My Story" has been developed especially for use with slow learners. You may not find it appropriate for all children because some may consider it rather personal. However, if the child is assured that his answers are only for the teacher, he will often be very revealing. I have used it with many children over a period of years. Many responses told nothing new, but a few offered real insight into the inner world of the child. I usually hand the paper back to the child and have him destroy it, although some teachers might want to preserve the forms.

If using this type of form offends you, or if you do not want the responsibility, you should ignore it. You may have techniques that work as well or better.

MY STORY

My name is _____ .

I live at _____ . My parents'

names are _____ .

I was born in _____ on the _____ day of

_____ 19 _____ . I am _____ years and

_____ months old. I am in the _____ grade

of _____ school.

There are _____ in my family. I

have _____ brothers and _____

sisters. We live in a _____ . We

have lived there _____ . I have attended

this school _____ years. Other schools I have

attended are _____ .

The subjects I like best in school are _____

_____ .

When I am home the things I like to do best are _____

_____

_____ .

The things I do not like to do at home are _____

_____ .

_____ . I help at home by _____

_____ . Sometimes I earn money by

_____ . When I get money I

_____ .

Things that make me happiest at home are _____

_____ . Things that make me unhappy

at home are _____ . I usually

sleep about _____hours each night. I (do, do not)

watch TV often at home. The kind of shows I like are _____

_____ . The games I

play outdoors are _____ . Indoor

games I like to play are _____ . We play at

_____ . At home I play games with _____

_____ . I (do, do not) like to be alone.

I (do, do not) enjoy reading books. I like to read _____

_____ . I (do, do not) use my library card.

Things I own all my own are _____

_____ . Since I was old enough to remember,

places I have visited are _____ .

Places I would like to go are _____ .

I would like to travel by _____ .

If I could, the things I would change at school would be _____

_____ . Things I

like best about school are _____

_____ .

Sometimes I wonder about _____

_____ . I am afraid of_____ . When I am

through school, I want to be _____ . I

want to do this because _____

_____ .

Right now if I could make three wishes, I would wish:

1. _____ .

2. _____ .

3. _____ .

Bibliography

BAKER, HARRY J. *Introduction to Exceptional Children.* New York: The Macmillan Company, 1947.

BALDWIN, JOSEPH. "Troubled Child—Troubled Family." *Elementary School Journal,* January 1968, pp. 172-179.

BEGGS, DAVID W., III. *Team Teaching: Bold New Venture.* Bloomington, Ind.: Indiana University Press, 1965.

BITTON, E. C., AND WINANS, J. M. *Growing from Infancy to Adulthood.* New York: Appleton-Century-Crofts, 1968.

COVERT, CATHY. "Mental Retardation." *Report of AMA Conference on Mental Retardation.* Chicago: American Medical Association, 1965.

CRARY, RYLAND, *Humanizing the School.* New York: Alfred A. Knopf, Inc., 1969.

CRATTY, BRYANT J. *Developmental Sequences in Perceptual Motor Tasks.* Freeport, N.Y.: Education Activities Inc., 1967.

CRUICKSHANK, WILLIAM N. et al. *Psychology of Exceptional Children and Youth.* Englewood Cliffs, N.J.: Prentice-Hall, Inc. Chapter 9, by G. Orville Johnson, pp. 448-483.

DUNN, LLOYD M. et al. *Exceptional Children in the Schools.* New York: Holt, Rinehart & Winston, Inc., 1967. Chapter 2, pp. 53-128, and Chapter 10, pp. 521-557.

EDUCATIONAL POLICIES COMMISSION AT NEA AND AASA. *Education for All American Children,* Vol. III, Washington, D.C.: NEA, 1948.

EDWARDS, MORTON. *Your Child Today.* New York: Simon & Schuster, Inc. (Pocket Books), 1960.

EKSTEIN, RUDOLF, AND MOTTO, ROSES L. *From Learning for Love to Love of Learning.* New York: Brunner/Mazel, Inc., 1969. Chapter 6, pp. 65-78, and Chapter 9, pp. 197-211.

ELLIOTT, FRANKLIN. "Shy Middle-graders." *Elementary School Journal,* March 1968, pp. 296-300.

ELSBREE, WILLARD S. *Pupil Progress in the Elementary School.* New York: Teachers College Press, 1949.

ESBENSEN, THORWALD. *Working with Individualized Instruction.* Belmont, Calif.: Fearon Publishers, 1968.

FRAZIER, ALEXANDER et al. *Educating the Children of the Poor.* Washington, D.C.: Association for Supervision and Curriculum Development, NEA, 1968.

————. *Early Childhood Education Today.* Washington, D.C.: Association for Supervision and Curriculum Development, NEA, 1968.

FROSTIG, MARIANNE, AND HORNE, DAVID. *The Frostig Program for the Development of Visual Perception.* Chicago: Follett Publishing Company, 1964.

GETMAN, G. N. *How to Develop Your Child's Intelligence.* Luverne, Minn.: Research Publications, 1962.

GINOTT, HAIM. *Between Parent and Child.* New York: The Macmillan Company, 1965.

GLASSER, WILLIAM. *Schools Without Failure.* New York: Harper & Row, Publishers, 1969.

GOLDSTEIN, HERBERT. *The Educable Mentally Retarded Child in the Elementary School.* What Research Says to the Teacher Series, no. 25. Association of Classroom Teachers, NEA, 1962.

GOODLAD, JOHN, AND ANDERSON, ROBERT H. *The Non-graded Elementary School.* New York: Harcourt Brace Jovanovich, Inc., 1963.

HABERMAN, M., AND RATHS, J. D. "High-Average-Low and What Makes Teachers Think So." *Elementary School Journal,* February 1968, pp. 241-245.

HASKEW, L. D., AND McLENDON, J. C. *This Is Teaching.* Glenview, Ill.: Scott, Foresman and Company, 1962.

HERMAN, WAYNE. *Principals' Guide to Teacher Personnel Problems in the Elementary School.* West Nyack, N.Y.: Parker Publishing Co., 1966.

HOLT, JOHN. *How Children Learn.* New York: Pitman Publishing Corp., 1967.

————. *The Underachieving School.* New York: Pitman Publishing Corp., 1969.

JENKINS, GLADYS; SCHACTER, HELEN; AND BANER, WILLIAM. *These Are Your Children.* Glenview, Ill.: Scott, Foresman and Company.

JOHNSON, ROBERT H., AND HUNT, JOHN. *Rx for Team Teaching.* Minneapolis, Minn.: Burgess Publishing Co., 1968.

JORDAN, THOMAS E. *The Mentally Retarded.* Columbus, Ohio: Charles E. Merrill Publishing Co., 1961.

KEHN, FREDA S., AND MINI, JOSEPH. *Let Children Be Children.* New York: Association Press, 1969.

KEPHART, NEWELL C. *The Slow Learner in the Classroom.* Columbus, Ohio: Charles E. Merrill Publishing Co., 1960.

KIRK, S. A., AND JOHNSON, G. O. *Educating the Retarded Child.* Boston: Houghton Mifflin Company, 1951.

LARRICK, NANCY. *A Parent's Guide to Children's Education.* New York: Simon & Schuster, Inc. (Pocket Books), 1964.

"LEARNING DISABILITIES—A SPECIAL REPORT." *Grade Teacher,* April 1970, pp. 48-64.

LEONARD, GEORGE B. *Education and Ecstasy.* New York: Delacorte Press, 1968.

LINDBERG, LUCILLE. *The Democratic Classroom.* New York: Bureau of Publications, Teachers College, Columbia University, 1954. Chapter 2, pp. 9-36, and Chapter 8, pp. 101-112.

RASMUSSEN, MARGARET et al. *Don't Push Me.* Washington, D.C.: Association for Childhood Education International, 1960.

————. *Individualizing Education.* Washington, D.C.: Association for Childhood Education International, 1964.

————. *Readings from Childhood Education.* Washington, D.C.: Association for Childhood Education International, 1966.

"Reaching the Disadvantaged." *Grade Teacher,* December 1968, pp. 43-78.

"The Right to Read." *Grade Teacher,* May-June 1970, pp. 53-152.

ROBINSON, H. B., AND ROBINSON, NANCY. *The Mentally Retarded Child—a Psychological Approach.* New York: McGraw-Hill Book Company, 1965.

ROGERS, CARL R. *Freedom To Learn.* Cleveland, Ohio: Charles E. Merrill Publishing Co., 1969. Chapter 4, pp. 103-127.

ROTHSTEIN, JEROME H., ed. *Mental Retardation—Readings and Resources.* New York: Holt, Rinehart & Winston, Inc., 1964. Chapter 4, pp. 136-162, and Chapter 5, pp. 163-284.

SCOBEY, MARY MARGARET, AND GRAHAM, GRACE, eds. *To Nurture Humaneness.* Washington, D.C.: Association for Supervision and Curriculum Development, NEA, 1970.

"Teaching with No Strings," *Grade Teacher,* November 1968, pp. 71-75.

THOMAS, JOHN. "Reconciling Theory and Practice in the Elementary School." *Elementary School Journal,* April 1968, pp. 349-352.

VALETT, ROBERT E. *Modifying Children's Behavior: A Guide for Parents and Professionals.* Belmont, Calif.: Fearon Publishers, 1969.

————. *Prescriptions for Learning: A Parent's Guide to Remedial Home Training.* Belmont, Calif.: Fearon Publishers, 1970.

————. *Programming Learning Disabilities.* Belmont, Calif.: Fearon Publishers, 1969.

————. *The Remediation of Learning Disabilities: A Handbook of Psychoeducational Resource Programs.* Belmont, Calif.: Fearon Publishers, 1967.

WICKS, FRANCES G. *The Inner World of Childhood.* New York: Appleton-Century-Crofts, 1966.

WILLIAMS, ROBERT. "On School Marks." *Elementary School Journal,* October 1968, pp. 1-6.

YOUNIE, WILLIAM C. *Instructional Approaches to Slow Learning.* New York: Teachers College Press, 1967.